PRAISE FOR
Crash: The Great Depression and the Fall and Rise of America

A New York Public Library Best Book
A Chicago Public Library Best Book
A *Booklist* Editors' Choice title
A Notable Social Studies Trade Book for Young People
An ALA Notable Children's Book
A Bank Street College Best Children's Book

"*Crash* does a great job of mixing personal stories with big-picture history, delivering a **compelling narrative about the Great Depression**—and about how Americans' reaction to it changed our country forever."
—**STEVE SHEINKIN**, National Book Award finalist and Newbery Honor author of *Bomb* and *Most Dangerous*

"In a forceful, fast-paced, and well-informed narrative, **Marc Favreau lets readers experience—no, live!—the worst economic collapse in US history**....An impressive and important work."
—**JIM MURPHY**, two-time Newbery Honor- and Robert F. Sibert Award-winning author of *An American Plague*

"*Crash* is **smart, thorough, visually engaging—and incredibly relevant**. I was riveted—I think people of any age who are interested in understanding American history, especially in order to understand where we are today, will be too."
—**KATE SCHATZ**, *New York Times* bestselling author of *Rad American Women A–Z*, *Rad Women Worldwide*, and *Rad Girls Can*

"*Crash* is a **terrific** book, chock-full of personal touches, details, and photographs that bring the people who lived through the Great Depression to life."
—**GEORGE O'CONNOR**, *New York Times* bestselling author of the Olympians graphic-novel series

"If you want to understand your grandparents' world into which they were born, thus affecting the world into which you were born, **READ THIS!**"
—**BILL MOYERS**, Emmy and Peabody Award–winning broadcast journalist and bestselling author

★ "A **dynamic** read deserving of a wide audience."
—*KIRKUS REVIEWS*, starred review

★ "Enlightening." —*BOOKLIST*, starred review

★ "*Crash* will deliver on all levels." —*VOYA*, starred review

Spies: The Secret Showdown Between America and Russia

A *New York Times* Best Children's Book of the Year
A *Publishers Weekly* Best Book of the Year
A Junior Library Guild selection

"Heart-stopping." —*THE NEW YORK TIMES BOOK REVIEW*

"*Spies* is narrative nonfiction at its finest: insightful, impeccably researched, and, most of all, **impossible to put down**."
—**DEBORAH HOPKINSON**, author of *Titanic: Voices from the Disaster*, a Sibert Honor Book

"It's hard to think of a book about espionage that is as **entertaining, accurate, and accessible** as *Spies*."
—**GREG MILLER**, Pulitzer Prize–winning national security correspondent for *The Washington Post*

"Marc Favreau's **endlessly engaging** book brings this dangerous struggle alive and will take his readers on a rollicking ride through the thrills, fears, and cliff-hanger contests of those tumultuous years."
—**JOHN McLAUGHLIN**, former acting director and deputy director of the CIA

★ *Publishers Weekly* ★ *Booklist*

Attacked! Pearl Harbor and the Day War Came to America

★ "A **jaw-dropping** account of Pearl Harbor....Artfully conceived and grippingly told." —***PUBLISHERS WEEKLY***, starred review

"An **inclusive, expansive take** on a pivotal historical moment. [Favreau] accessibly and engagingly shows readers that with Pearl Harbor, the real story is 'more complicated—and much more interesting, tragic, and heroic—than the simplified version.'"
—***KIRKUS REVIEWS***

By Marc Favreau

Crash: The Great Depression and the Fall and Rise of America

Spies: The Secret Showdown Between America and Russia

Attacked! Pearl Harbor and the Day War Came to America

By Michael Eric Dyson and Marc Favreau

Unequal: A Story of America

Represent: The Unfinished Fight for the Vote

CRASH

CRA

THE GREAT DEPRESSION AND

LB

LITTLE, BROWN AND COMPANY
New York Boston

ISH

THE FALL AND RISE OF AMERICA

Marc Favreau

Little, Brown and Company
Hachette Book Group
1290 Avenue of the Americas, New York, NY 10104
Visit us at LBYR.com

Originally published in hardcover and ebook by Little, Brown and Company in April 2018
First Trade Paperback Edition: May 2024

Little, Brown and Company is a division of Hachette Book Group, Inc.
The Little, Brown name and logo are registered trademarks of Hachette Book Group, Inc.

The publisher is not responsible for websites (or their content) that are not owned by the publisher.

Image credits can be found throughout.

Little, Brown and Company books may be purchased in bulk for business, educational, or promotional
use. For information, please contact your local bookseller or the Hachette Book Group Special Markets
Department at special.markets@hbgusa.com.

The Library of Congress has cataloged the hardcover edition as follows:
Names: Favreau, Marc, 1968– author.
Title: Crash : the Great Depression and the fall and rise of America / Marc Favreau.
Description: First edition. | New York : Little, Brown Books for Young Readers, 2018.
Identifiers: LCCN 2016056930| ISBN 9780316545860 (hardback) | ISBN 9780316464895 (library edition
ebook) | ISBN 9780316545839 (ebook)
Subjects: LCSH: United States—History—1933–1945—Juvenile literature. | United States—
History—1919–1933—Juvenile literature. | Depressions, 1929—United States—Juvenile literature. |
New Deal, 1933–1939—Juvenile literature. | United States—Economic conditions—1918–1945—Juvenile
literature. | United States—History—1933–1945—Sources—Juvenile literature. | United States—
History—1919–1933—Sources—Juvenile literature. | Depressions, 1929—United States—Sources—
Juvenile literature. | New Deal, 1933–1939—Sources—Juvenile literature. | United States—Economic
conditions—1918–1945—Sources—Juvenile literature. | BISAC: JUVENILE NONFICTION / History / United
States / 20th Century. | JUVENILE NONFICTION / Social Issues / Homelessness & Poverty. | JUVENILE
NONFICTION / Business & Economics. | JUVENILE NONFICTION / Social Issues / Prejudice & Racism. |
JUVENILE NONFICTION / People & Places / United States / General.
Classification: LCC E806 .F269   2017 | DDC 973.91—dc23
LC record available at https://lccn.loc.gov/2016056930

ISBNs: 978-0-316-54587-7 (pbk.), 978-0-316-54583-9 (ebook)

Printed in the United States of America

CCR

10 9 8 7 6 5 4 3 2 1

For my mom, who taught me to be
curious about the world around me,
and for my dad, who gave me
the history bug

CONTENTS

PROLOGUE

America did not see it coming.

In 1929, the United States was riding high on a great bubble of energy and excitement sometimes called the "Roaring Twenties." Radios blared music in living rooms and dance halls; champagne and gin—both illegal—flowed freely in "speakeasy" clubs; and young men and women everywhere practiced the newest dance steps late into the evenings.

Most people worked six days a week and made enough money to afford refrigerators, toasters, irons, and other new gadgets rolling off new factory assembly lines. The Ford Model T, a symbol of America's energetic, on-the-move lifestyle, clogged highways and parking lots.

For many, life was getting easier. People felt that a new kind of prosperity had arrived—the kind that would stick around forever.

The most thrilling show of the decade was on narrow Wall Street, in downtown Manhattan at the New York Stock Exchange, a place where the wealthy could gamble with the millions of dollars piling up in their bank accounts. There they traded stocks, or pieces of paper representing shares of companies that were for sale to the public.

In the heyday of the 1920s stock market, stock prices spiraled upward as more and more buyers jumped in, willing to bet that what they bought today would increase in value by tomorrow. Year after year, they were right: From 1922 to 1929, the average stock price more than quadrupled.

People did not actually earn any real money until they sold their stocks to someone else and then pocketed the difference between the purchase price and the selling price. Yet who would ever think of selling, when the value of stocks—the price someone else was willing to pay—kept going up?

Then, like a stone tossed into the air that finally obeys the laws of gravity, the stock market paused. One by one, Wall Street's investors sensed the change in the air and decided that, finally, it might be time to sell off their stocks—before the value dropped.

It didn't happen all at once. But by the end of October, panic gripped the stock market. Whereas just a few months earlier everyone was buying, now all anyone could think of was to sell, sell, sell. So many shares of stock were sold on Black Tuesday, October 29, 1929, that the ticker-tape machines—which recorded the sales on spools of paper—could not keep up, and continued to run late into the night.

Shouts and fistfights broke out on the usually civilized floor of the New York Stock Exchange. In a few short hours, as the day came to a close, businessmen and investors saw their entire fortunes wiped out. Several even committed suicide by leaping to their deaths from the skyscrapers towering above Wall Street.

Newspapers all over the country landed on stoops the following morning, with the dark news from Wall Street: The Crash had come to America.

The force of the Crash shook America's confidence in the future. Even those who had no money invested in the market felt stung by the news from New York. If wealthy investors could lose their fortunes in a day, what could happen to them? As the country approached a new decade—the 1930s—millions of Americans decided to hang on to what little money they had.

A nation of consumers became a nation of savers. Commerce screeched to a halt.

By the end of 1929, Americans sensed that a change was coming. But what happened next quickly exceeded even their darkest predictions.

PART ONE

FALL

We lived in a shack by the railroad tracks in Phoenix. It was so bad that they couldn't rent it to someone else, so they didn't even charge us rent. We scrounged for food, I'll tell you we scrounged for food.

—WILLIAM WIGHT, DESCRIBING LIFE IN THE EARLY 1930s

Impoverished children from Oklahoma, in a migrant worker camp in California, living in their family's truck.
Dorothea Lange, photographer, Library of Congress, Farm Security Administration/Office of War Information Collection, 1936

CHAPTER ONE
DYSTOPIA, USA

The worst calamity ever to strike the United States of America was not an explosion, a plague, an earthquake, or even the invasion of a foreign army. It wasn't really even an "event." It didn't happen suddenly, or all at once; rather, it was like an avalanche on a snow-covered mountain, one that begins quietly, accelerates quickly, and soon swallows everything in its path. Not everyone noticed what was happening at first, and some people who did notice—for example, US president Herbert Hoover, who took office in March 1929—denied what was really going on. By then, it was much too late.

You couldn't point to it, see it, or touch it. But few people in the United States of America escaped its effects. Although most people have forgotten about it today, the Great Depression of the 1930s turned an entire generation of Americans upside down.

The word *depression* has different meanings. It comes from the Latin for "pressing down" and is often used to describe a kind of mental illness, when someone suffers from a gloomy view of the world and of the future. These definitions are close cousins to the term that describes what happened to the US economy in the 1930s.

The Great Depression was a severe economic downturn, or "slump." The US economy had gone through sharp economic downturns—and even several depressions—before the 1930s. The Great Depression was different, both more destructive and longer-lasting than any other.

As the new year dawned in 1930, the effects of the Crash on Wall Street caught up with people living on Main Streets from Oakland, California, to Wilmington, Delaware. The US economy, for the first time in memory, was grinding to halt.

A vicious circle closed in on itself, as fewer people working meant less money spent on the things that factories made, causing factories to reduce production or close altogether—leading to more layoffs, month after month. Big numbers tell part of this story: Barely nine months after Black Tuesday, the number of people out of work in the United States had *tripled*. General Motors, one of the largest companies in the United States, employed 260,000 men and women in 1929; eighteen months after the Crash, the company had laid off more than 100,000 of these workers. Detroit, home to the biggest auto manufacturers in the world, was especially hard hit: In 1930, the city produced two million fewer cars than it had in 1929. Ford Motor Company closed its River Rouge plant in Detroit, throwing 60,000 people out of work. In Chicago, the unemployment rate—the percentage of people who wanted to work but could not find jobs—approached 50 percent. By 1932, roughly one-quarter of all American workers had lost their jobs.

An unemployed man in Detroit in 1930.

James Franco was a teenager when the stock market crash rocked New York City. But he and his family lived far away, in San Diego, California, overlooking the Pacific Ocean. "I remember the paper-boys screaming about the stock market crash and that sort of thing," James said, "but it just went in one ear and out the other...I could care less what was happening on Wall Street, or knew less."

James and his family had emigrated from Greece in the 1920s, when he was only seven years old. They knew what it meant to be poor; his father had scraped by as a fisherman in Greece, and had moved the family to America in search of a better life.

The Francos prospered in California. James tasted ice cream for the first time when he was eleven years old—he couldn't believe the "almost miraculous environment" that he found himself in. His father owned a wholesale fish market that sold seafood to restaurants in San Diego. They weren't rich but they enjoyed a comfortable, stable life in their adopted country.

The first aftershocks of the Crash caught up with the Franco family in the spring of 1930. With each passing week, the number of people in San Diego eating out at restaurants dwindled, and that meant restaurants stopped buying fish from the Francos' family business. James's father soon felt the pinch, and "he couldn't pay his own bills so that was it," James remembered. By June, his dad was back to working as a fisherman—the very job he had left Greece to escape.

But it wasn't until late that summer, when he asked his father a simple question, that the full truth of his family's predicament became clear. "I remember one day approaching my dad and asking him for seventy-five cents that I needed," Franco recalled later. "He had a strange look in his eyes I had never seen before—a kind of agonizing look. And he said...'Well there's no more money, Jimmy...all we have now is to worry about how we are going to eat...'"

It was a devastating descent for the Franco family. "I could read the expression of agony in my parents' eyes," James recalled, "and really realize that a way of life had suddenly ended."

Like millions of families all over America, the Francos now lived in a world of uncertainty and fear, as bills piled up and income shrank. James came home from school one day to find a sign posted in his front yard. Because his mother could not read English, she had waited for James to explain it to her. The note contained a terrifying message: "We were actually going to be evicted and thrown in the streets."

That time, the Francos were able to cobble together enough money to hold on to their house. But life became filled with "small crises," James recalled, such as "the day the gas was shut off [and] my mother had to cook in the backyard over an open fire."

The Francos considered themselves lucky. They didn't go hungry. They held the family together, under a single roof, through the worst days of the Depression.

As winter approached in 1930, more and more Americans were not so lucky. Money quickly ran out as the weeks and months ticked by, for the employed and unemployed alike. At first, people cut back on luxury items, skipping dinners at restaurants and having shoes repaired instead of buying a new pair. In Detroit, Michigan, movie theaters that could hold a thousand spectators sold no more than a few dozen tickets at a time. In Ypsilanti, Michigan, Virginia Davis-Brown's father "went hunting almost every day for food and he would come home with squirrels and rabbits and raccoons." She remembered that her mother, Helen, "would can anything that he brought home, so we would have enough food to carry us through in the winter, because there was no money." Violet Krall, who grew up near Milwaukee, Wisconsin, took her lunch to school in those early days of the Depression. "Once," she recalled, "as I was beginning to eat my egg salad sandwich, the girl in the seat next to mine said, 'You must be rich.' I asked her why she said that, and she said that they could not afford eggs."

Far away from the big cities, there were reports of people eating wild berries and dandelions scavenged from fields, just to stay alive. In West Virginia, schoolteachers began to notice that their students looked thin and gaunt, and were unable to focus. A school administrator in Chicago worried that "every day we have children who come to school without breakfast and who state that they have nothing to eat in their homes." In Texas, the strain of hunger during Vera Criswell's pregnancy passed to her third daughter, born in June 1931, who suffered from severe digestive illnesses. "I didn't have the food I should have when I was carrying her," Criswell remembered, adding that her baby "was a direct product of the Depression."

In some cases, gnawing hunger provoked acts of desperation. Farmers near the town of England, Arkansas, piled into their trucks on the morning of January 3, 1931, and staged a "food riot" in the center of town, threatening to break into the local grocery stores. One of these men, a farmer named Coney, offered this explanation to a reporter: "We all got pretty low on food here, and some was a-starvin'. Mebbe I was a little better fixed than most, 'cause we still had some food left. But when a woman comes over to me a-cryin'

In 1931, soup lines such as this one in Chicago became a common sight.
National Archives and Records Administration

and tells me her kids hain't et' nothin' fer two days, and grabs me and says, 'Coney, what are we a-goin' to do?' then somethin' went up in my head. I just says, 'Lady, you wait here. I'm a-goin' to get some food.'"

Lines for bread and soup formed at mealtimes in nearly every city and town in 1931. In New York City, nearly one hundred thousand people got their daily meals from one of several hundred breadlines. And as the *New-York Evening Post* reported, every type of person could be found in need of free food: "There are laborers, carpenters, roofers, bakers, foremen, engineers, toolmakers, railroad workers, waiters, cooks, pantrymen, cigar makers, metal polishers, bricklayers, pipefitters, garage men, chauffeurs. There are common laborers, men with trades and men of the white collar class...shaved and equipped with clean linen."

When not enough money could be scrounged together, some families were even forced to abandon their homes.

In 1928, a laborer in Cleveland, Ohio, named John Sparenga purchased a home for his family at 11413 Lardet Avenue, a tree-lined street of neat wooden houses with covered front porches. With steady work and a good income, Sparenga kept up monthly mortgage payments on the $8,300 home loan he had taken out from a local bank. In the 1920s, Cleveland had become the nation's fifth-largest city, its huge steel and iron mills attracting thousands of new workers from all over the world, including many from Poland, Ukraine, Germany, Italy, and Hungary (where John's parents had immigrated from in the late nineteenth century). New neighborhoods, like the one on Lardet Avenue, sprung up all over the city, and for the first time, ordinary people like the Sparengas were able to taste success and comfort in America.

By 1930, Cleveland's mills and factories sputtered amid the first shocks of the economic slump. John Sparenga lost his job that year, and he soon fell behind on his house payments. Three years later, in 1933, he could barely afford to feed his family and was depending almost completely on donations from a local charity. Finally, the bank foreclosed on his property and moved to evict John, his wife, and their four children. On a hot summer morning, on July 28, sheriff's deputies showed up at the Sparengas' door to carry their furniture and other belongings out onto the street.

A cloud of tear gas rises up in front of the Sparengas' house in Cleveland, Ohio, in 1933.

The Sparenga family's eviction was too much for their neighbors, who knew that any of them might suffer the same fate. A crowd formed to stop the deputies from carrying out the eviction. Bricks and bottles flew. By the end of the day, as word spread throughout the city, 5,000 angry people surrounded the house, scuffling and battling with more than 150 police officers. The police used tear gas and fire hoses against the demonstrators, who fell back and then regrouped four times throughout the night. A newspaper reporter covering the scene wrote that "this is a crowd that won't scatter, a crowd that is strangely grim and determined."

In the end, the police pushed the protesters back. The Sparenga family lost their home, and there is no record of where they ended up.

The Sparengas were not an isolated case. Everywhere, adult children moved in with their parents, families doubled up to share expenses, or children were sent to live with grandparents. Lacking enough money to pay their rents, Americans moved into cars, caves, or makeshift shacks built of any scraps they could find. Stella Dean's family of four lived in a truck, traveling from town to town in search of food and work. "You don't know what the heat is like in the Southwest until you've been out there cooped up in a truck on the road in the summer," she recalled. "The dust out on the fields glimmer with the glare of the sun until your eyeballs burned just to look at it, and after a while it all'd look like an endless lake." Mary Owsley of Oklahoma City knew of one family, "a man and a woman and seven children lived in a hole in the

A homeless man asleep in his shack near downtown Seattle in October 1931.
James Patrick Lee, photographer, University of Washington Libraries, Special Collections

ground. You'd be surprised how nice it was, how nice they kept it. They had chairs and tables and beds back up in that hole. And they had the dirt all braced up there, just like a cave."

As a last, desperate measure, some people simply walked away. "Hoboes" became a common sight on street corners and back alleys across the country. The term originated in California in the 1890s but entered everyday language during the Depression (possibly as an abbreviation of "homeless boy" or "homeward bound"). Hoboes were simply men, women, and thousands upon thousands of children, looking for work and shelter, riding on freight trains and sleeping in open fields and on roadsides all over the United States.

In Michigan, Virginia Davis-Brown remembered "men who walked up Michigan Avenue coming from Chicago and going to Detroit that had no food and they would stop at certain houses. My mother always had an egg sandwich for them and they always said, 'thank you,' and wanted to help. Sometimes they'd see if they could help do something around the house to pay for what they had received and then they would continue on their way." For the most part, a hobo's goal was always the same: a day's work, a little bit of money socked away for family back home, sometimes even a hot meal. It's likely that several million Americans wandered far away from home in the early years of the Depression, in search of work.

Two unemployed men walking along a highway in California.
Dorothea Lange, photographer, Library of Congress, Farm Security Administration/Office of War Information Collection, 1937

The most popular song of 1931 was "Brother, Can You Spare a Dime?," by songwriter Yip Harburg and composer Jay Gorney. Describing the life of a homeless drifter who was once "always there right on the job," the song captured a hard truth of that year: In 1931, hoboes were a living sign that communities were unraveling.

Slept in a paper box. Bummed swell breakfast three eggs and four pieces of meat. Hit [up] guy in big car in front of garage. Cop told me to scram. Rode freight to Roessville. Small burg, but got dinner. Walked Bronson. [...] Rode to Sidell. [...] Hit homes for meals and turned down. Had to buy supper 20 cents. Raining.

—DIARY ENTRY, SEPTEMBER 10, 1932, FROM A YOUNG BOY NAMED "BLINK"

This fourteen-year-old boy was living in a migrant camp near Sacramento, California. He survived for two days on frozen tomatoes from a field nearby. His father said, "They call me a road hog and a bum; but if I am, how did that boy get into the eighth grade?"
Dorothea Lange, photographer, Library of Congress, Farm Security Administration/Office of War Information Collection, 1936

————•◆•————

Surviving the loss of a job or clinging to a home often depended on one thing: a savings account at a bank. During the boom years of the 1920s, many people had set aside extra money, either for retirement or to tide them over during lean times. For these people, the Depression's final blow was also its most devastating.

Even before the Crash, American banks were shaky institutions. Most did not have enough money in their vaults to cover what they owed to all of their depositors at any given time. Normally this system worked. But when rumors began to circulate that the banks were on the verge of collapsing, account holders stampeded to local banks to collect their money, in what became known as "bank runs." In many cases, the money simply wasn't there.

The first bank to collapse was the National Bank of Kentucky in Louisville, which abruptly locked its doors on November 17, 1930. The news spread like an electric charge, and panicked depositors withdrew money from banks all across the state and beyond.

Raymond Tarver of Dublin, Georgia, worked at the First National Bank, one of the biggest businesses in town. Before the Depression, Tarver considered himself a success story. He and his wife "really began at the bottom," he said, living with his parents, saving their

After taking this photograph, Dorothea Lange recorded the following notes: "After a lift of five miles by a passing motorist, this family of homeless, walking people are left at the edge of the next town."
Dorothea Lange, photographer, Library of Congress, Farm Security Administration/Office of War Information Collection, 1939

In New York City, the Bank of the United States went out of business on December 11, 1930, almost without warning. Its account holders were mostly Jewish immigrants, who worked long hours in the city's garment industry (the bank was known informally as the "Pantspressers' Bank"). At that institution alone, the life savings of more than four hundred thousand people were wiped out in a single day.
National Archives and Records Administration, 1931

pennies, and growing vegetables in their spare time to sell for extra money. Eventually Tarver earned enough at his bank job to afford his own home, along with a Ford Model T. He kept his extra earnings in a savings account at First National Bank.

One morning, an unexpected phone call interrupted the Tarver family breakfast. It was a fellow employee from the bank, with panic in his voice.

"Tarver, have you heard the news?"

The First National Bank had locked its doors. Nobody knew what was going on, but—with news of bank runs all over the state—Tarver feared the worst.

Tarver rushed into town, "and, sure enough," he recalled, "in front of the bank there stood a crowd of employees, as blank expressions on their faces as I've ever seen."

First National was not only a pillar of the Dublin community but was one of the last banks standing in town, after a series of bank runs earlier that year. "Everybody thought their money was safe," according to Tarver. And for him, it was a double blow: Both his savings *and* his job were on the line.

"We worked on at the bank, trying to get things in shape," Tarver recalled, "with no hopes deep down in our hearts of ever opening up again." Layoff notices arrived one by one, and Tarver's came a few days later. "My job was gone and my savings too."

It was a terrible time in Dublin. Tarver remembered that "there were thousands who went down during the panic—lost fortunes, homes, businesses, and in fact everything."

For ordinary people, from Dublin, Georgia, to Detroit, Michigan, a bank failure was a shattering experience. When a bank went out of business, its depositors had no recourse; they simply lost their money. At the shuttered Binga State Bank on the South Side of Chicago, a mostly African American neighborhood, the *Chicago Defender* news-paper reported that "crowds of depositors gathered in front of the bank. Two uniformed policeman were out on guard for several days. There were no disorders. Instead, there was a deathlike pall that hung over those who had entrusted their life savings to Binga...." Dempsey Travis, who was ten in the summer of 1930 when the Binga State Bank collapsed, blamed the bank for his beloved uncle's death: "Thrifty Uncle Otis became destitute with the turn of the examiner's key in the front door of the bank. Otis Travis died in 1933, broke and broken-hearted, without having recovered one penny of his savings."

A bank run at the Erie National Bank of Philadelphia in 1931, with depositors lined up around the block, hoping to withdraw money from their accounts.
Philadelphia Record Collection, Historical Society of Pennsylvania

All told, more than nine thousand banks failed across the country, nearly *one-third* of all banks in the United States. In some areas, the percentages were even higher: In the Chicago region, more than 80 percent of all banks were wiped out during the Great Depression.

To try to protect banks that had not yet collapsed, governors in thirty-two states declared "bank holidays," forbidding people from taking any more money out of their accounts—simply because banks did not have enough money left in their vaults to cover all of their customers' deposits.

Nothing like this had ever happened in America. The nation's money supply had simply dried up.

With so little real cash in circulation, some towns created different kinds of "scrip," a fake currency that could be used to buy and sell necessities at local stores, restaurants, and other businesses. Scrip (a word that refers to an IOU written on a piece of paper) was little more than invented money, a last-ditch effort to keep businesses in operation.

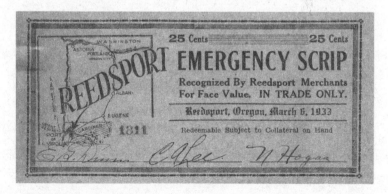

"Scrip" that could be used in Reedsport, Oregon, during the Depression.
Oregon State University Libraries Digital Collections, 1933

In Pismo Beach, California, residents could use "clamshell scrip" with eleven local stores, with each shell representing one dollar. The National Numismatic Collection, Smithsonian Institution, National Museum of American History, 1933

On November 12, 1931, Benjamin Roth recorded in his diary a haunting description of his hometown of Youngstown, Ohio, conjuring up images that could have described thousands of communities across the United States:

> Things remain at a standstill. There is no money in circulation, the stores and business places are deserted, and everybody seems to have given up their initiative.

After a downward slide lasting nearly two years, the worst crisis of unemployment and mass poverty in history now had the United States firmly in its grip.

When an avalanche reaches the bottom, an eerie quiet sets in, as survivors get their bearings and take stock of injuries. After the first year of the Great Depression, Americans awoke to this kind of stunned silence. The institutions they had once looked to for support—workplaces, banks, and even homes—had failed. People everywhere now wanted answers from the one person with the power to do something to help.

J. Huffman of Grassy Butte, North Dakota, sits in front of his closed store, "waiting for better times."
Arthur Rothstein, photographer, Library of Congress, Farm Security Administration/Office of War Information Collection, 1937

CHAPTER TWO
THE UNLUCKIEST PRESIDENT

In the early days of the Depression, Americans expressed relief that someone as competent as Herbert Hoover was sitting in the Oval Office.

Before becoming president, Hoover had earned a reputation for calm, expert leadership as secretary of commerce under Presidents Warren G. Harding and Calvin Coolidge. In 1920, Franklin Delano Roosevelt (who would later succeed Hoover as president) gushed that "Hoover is certainly a wonder....I wish we could make him President of the United States. There could not be a better one." Many viewed Hoover as the nation's best-qualified public servant.

Herbert Hoover believed that he had earned every ounce of his reputation. Born and raised in an austere Quaker community in Iowa, Hoover learned the hard way about getting ahead. His mother was a Quaker minister and his father a blacksmith; he remembered

Herbert Hoover as a senior at Leland Stanford Junior University, in 1894–95.
The Herbert Hoover Presidential Library–Museum, National Archives and Records Administration

long hours spent in strict religious services, seated on a hard bench. Hoover became an orphan at a young age, and passed a difficult, lonely childhood with different relatives—first in a sod house on the South Dakota frontier, and then with an uncle in Oregon who forced him to do heavy chores six days a week (he attended church on the seventh). Later in life, Hoover developed an interest in food, something he attributed to his childhood experiences—because he "was always hungry then."

Herbert Hoover eventually broke free from his uncle and entered the first class at Leland Stanford, a new university in California. He was the youngest student in the school. A professor at Stanford remarked that Hoover "put his teeth together with great decision, and his whole face and posture showed his determination to pass...at any cost."

After graduation, Hoover secured a job at the local office of a mining company, the first step in a career that would change his destiny. He traveled the world as a mining engineer, rapidly proving himself a tough manager and a skillful businessman. By the age of thirty-six, Hoover was a self-made millionaire, running a global mining empire. He retired a wealthy man, at thirty-eight, in 1912.

Yet with the outbreak of World War I, in 1914, Hoover opened a new chapter in his life, as—like many Americans—he read the daily reports of starvation and devastation in Europe. He was especially shocked by the news of women and children suffering in Belgium, following the invasion of the German Army. Entirely on his own initiative, Hoover created an organization, the Commission for Relief in Belgium, which succeeded in keeping four million people from starving.

It was an enormously complicated operation, involving hundreds of boats, thousands of tons of supplies moved through a dangerous war zone, and delicate negotiations with warring powers. In the end, one historian described Hoover's efforts as "the greatest humanitarian undertaking the world had ever seen."

Food stacked high, for distribution to war refugees in Europe, 1916.
The Herbert Hoover Presidential Library–Museum, National Archives and Records Administration

By the end of the war, Hoover had built a sterling record as a dogged administrator and an effective leader. He strongly believed that individual self-reliance, combined with private charity, was the key to solving public problems. Hoover's childhood experiences convinced him that anyone, no matter what his or her circumstances, could succeed. His later achievements in World War I and in government persuaded him that the government's role was to stay out of the way, and to intervene only as a last resort. He was not alone: Many people, from all walks of life, believed that American freedom was freedom *from* government interference.

The booming economy of the 1920s seemed to validate Hoover's worldview. In 1928, as the Republican Party's candidate for president, he won the highest political office in the land in a decisive victory.

Newspaper headlines heaped praise upon Hoover, with one going so far as to call him "the most useful American citizen now alive." Hoover wondered openly whether America's enthusiasm for him had gotten out of hand. "I have no dread of the ordinary work of the presidency," he said to a newspaper editor in January 1929. "What I do fear is the...exaggerated idea the people have conceived of me. They have a conviction that I am a sort of superman, that no problem is beyond my capacity...." And in what ended up being alarmingly prescient, he added, "If some unprecedented calamity should come upon the nation...I would be sacrificed to the unreasoning disappointment of a people who expected too much."

That disappointment arrived much sooner than anyone could have guessed.

Herbert Hoover, thirty-first president of the United States, 1929–1933, pictured with his dog, King Tut, in 1930.

The Great Depression was not Herbert Hoover's fault, but he ended up getting a lot of the blame for making it worse. Behind the scenes, Hoover worked late into the night in the White House, drafting letters to charities such as the Red Cross, urging them to expand their donation programs for the unemployed. There was one thing, though, that Herbert Hoover refused to do: use the power of the federal government to help people directly. Hoover believed that the economy would fix itself, so doing nothing was no accident in Hoover's White House, it was official policy. He was convinced that, thanks to his hands-off policies, the tide of depression would turn—eventually. "Our measures and policies have demonstrated their effectiveness," he proclaimed as late as 1932, as the nation approached its third year of the Depression. "They have preserved the American people from certain chaos. They have preserved a final fortress of stability in the world."

Unfortunately for Hoover—and for all Americans—the Great Depression was far from over.

By the end of 1932, few Americans could find anything nice to say about Herbert Hoover. The cowboy comedian Will Rogers joked, "If someone bit an apple and found a worm in it, Hoover would get the blame."

As the nation spiraled downward, Hoover's reputation tumbled

One of many newspaper cartoons that began to appear, as Hoover failed to solve the nation's economic crisis. In the 1930s, political cartoons such as this conveyed important political messages to masses of people.

[First name unknown] Tulley, Princeton University Archives, 1932 with it. The president's face appeared in public mainly as a cartoon caricature. In private, he looked haggard and overworked. American slang found dozens of uses for Hoover's name, including Hoovervilles (homeless camps), Hoover flags (empty pants pockets, pulled out to show that someone had no money), Hoover blankets (newspapers used by homeless people to cover themselves at night), and Hoover wagons (any car or truck that had to be pulled by horses or mules).

Signs criticizing Herbert Hoover at a "Hooverville" camp, 1932.
National Archives and Records Administration

Hooverville post office sign, Seattle, Washington, from the early 1930s.
Museum of History and Industry, Seattle, MOHAI, 1980.7029.1

In the winter of 1932, a journalist observed a change in the nation's mood, noting that "there is throughout the country a stirring among the unemployed such as we have not witnessed before, certainly not in the present period of depression....They are at last reaching the point where they can no longer endure the hardships of unemployment and haphazard charity." If the president wasn't going to do anything, some Americans decided to join together and take matters into their own hands.

Led by the nation's military veterans, these men and women soon became known as the Bonus Army.

In 1924, the US Congress had passed a law, the World War Adjusted Compensation Act, granting bonuses to American soldiers who had fought in World War I. (American troops had fought in Europe from

1917 to 1918.) The law awarded these veterans $1.25 for every day they had fought overseas, and $1.00 for every day they had served on the home front, in the United States. The catch was that the payment of the bonuses would not be paid until 1945, to give the US Treasury time to accrue the necessary funds, which totaled over $3.5 billion, or over $50 billion in today's dollars. In the meantime, each veteran was given an Adjusted Service Certificate, which reflected the amount he was owed, plus interest.

The mass unemployment and suffering brought on by the Depression inspired many veterans to demand early payment of their bonus, to help them through the difficult years. Some members of Congress supported their claims. Other national leaders—including Herbert Hoover—strongly opposed the idea, arguing that the nation would have to raise taxes to pay for the bonuses, something that in their view might harm the economy even more.

Thousands of these veterans, along with their families, decided to take their case directly to Washington, DC. Led by a former Army sergeant named Walter W. Waters, they formed the Bonus Army (or the Bonus

A flyer advertising the Bonus March of 1932.
Rare Book and Special Collections Division, Library of Congress

Expeditionary Force, a play on the name of the American force that fought in World War I), whose mission was to march on Washington and force the government to pay up.

With no jobs and little hope, but a fierce sense that the government *owed* them for their service, the Bonus Army marchers came from all directions, riding the trains and stopping in towns all across the country, often to the cheers of crowds that met them at stations.

The Bonus Army camp in Anacostia Flats, Washington, DC, in 1932.
Harris & Ewing, photographer, Library of Congress, Prints and Photographs Division

Twenty thousand men, women, and children streamed into Washington, DC, that spring. Poverty-stricken but determined, they set up temporary camps in vacant lots and abandoned buildings.

Several thousand people camped in a large open area in Anacostia, just across the river from the capital. With the support of police chief Pelham Glassford, who sympathized with the marchers, the Anacostia camp soon transformed into a mini-city, with a post office, street signs, and community kitchens.

Bonus Army protesters on the lawn of the US Capitol in 1932.
Library of Congress, Prints and Photographs Division, Theodor Horydczak Collection

The veterans rallied in front of the Capitol. They marched in peaceful protest in the streets of Washington. They made sure that the nation's leaders could not ignore the victims of the Great Depression.

Herbert Hoover, however, was not sympathetic. And after years of inaction, the president made a fateful decision to *act*.

On Thursday, July 28, Hoover ordered Army units to fan across the city and eject the Bonus Army from its camps. General Douglas MacArthur personally commanded the operation, which included cavalry, tanks, and soldiers with fixed bayonets. Tear gas burned people's eyes—and bullets whizzed through the air. Scenes of unbelievable violence and mayhem played out only a short distance from the White House and the Capitol building. "Veterans were packing and rushing about," recalled Elbridge Purdy, who witnessed the battle. "Tear gas, which was being used to drive them out, made it difficult to see....It was like riding through the steam of a teakettle." The nation's capital was suddenly transformed into a war zone.

General Douglas MacArthur, who later became a hero during World War II, leads the effort to evict the Bonus Army marchers from Washington, DC, in July 1932.
Library of Congress, Prints and Photographs Division

Bonus Army shacks burn to the ground in Anacostia Flats, 1932. A newspaper
reporter who witnessed the event wrote, "I watched the soldiers moving from hut
to hut, starting the blaze. Shanty after shanty went up in flames, along with the
meager belongings of the vets and their families."

Records of the Office of the Chief Signal Officer, Photographs of American Military Activities, National Archives
and Records Administration

On the morning of July 29, 1932, a thick, acrid cloud of smoke
hung over Washington, and newspapers everywhere carried headlines about Hoover's attack on the Bonus Army. A veteran of World
War I had been killed, and nearly sixty other men and women were
wounded in the skirmishes.

President Hoover quickly realized that he had to tell his side of the
story and salvage what remained of his reputation. "In order to put
an end to this rioting and defiance of civil authority," he proclaimed,

"I have asked the Army to assist the District authorities to restore order." Unfortunately for Hoover, the Bonus Army veterans, and much of the nation, saw matters quite differently.

> There was an old Hoover
> Who Lived in a Shoe.
> He had so many veterans
> He didn't know what to do.
> So he gassed them and tanked them.
> And burned up their beds
> And then told all the people
> The vets were all Reds.
> —*B.E.F. NEWS*, SEPTEMBER 17, 1932

There was little question in most people's minds about where the blame lay for the violence. "Every drop of blood shed today...can be laid directly on the threshold of the White House," wrote Walter W. Waters.

Newspapers around the country carried photographs of burning shacks and plumes of black smoke coiling above the city. These shocking images communicated a loud message: Herbert Hoover had no idea how to solve the Great Depression. From outside of Washington, DC, it seemed to Americans that the nation's capital was burning out of control. In the final months of Hoover's presidency, his philosophy of government, along with his reputation, went up in smoke.

As the nation reeled from news of the attack on the Bonus Army, and sank more deeply into the Depression, the coming presidential election took on greater urgency. What could be done to fix America's broken economy? And who had the strength and the know-how to cut through the uncertainty?

The Democratic nominee for president of the United States, Franklin Delano Roosevelt, had begun to tinker with practical solutions to poverty, unemployment, and the economic crisis during his time as governor of New York, the nation's most populous state. Roosevelt knew that it was beyond the power of individual people, working alone, to climb their way out of the Great Depression. He believed in the positive power of government—and, above all, he believed in *action*. Roosevelt's fundamental approach to the Great Depression could not have contrasted more with Hoover's. Help for people stricken by the Crash, he declared, "must be extended by Government, not as a matter of charity, but as a matter of social duty; the State accepts the task cheerfully because it believes that it will help restore that close relationship with its people which is necessary to preserve our democratic form of government."

On Election Day in November 1932, Americans made it clear that they were ready for Franklin Delano Roosevelt—and done with Hoover. FDR won a sweeping victory, carrying all but six states— including many that had not swung toward a Democratic candidate

RETURN THE GOVERNMENT TO THE PEOPLE!
ON NOVEMBER 8th.

He's Ready!   Are You?

WE NEED ACTION!

**FROM
PRESIDENT HOOVER'S
ACCEPTANCE SPEECH**
August 11, 1928.

"We in America today are nearer to the final triumph over poverty than ever before in the history of any land. The poorhouse is vanishing from among us. We have not yet reached the goal, but given a chance to go forward with the policies of the last eight years (Harding and Coolidge), and we shall soon, with the help of God, be in sight of the day when poverty will be banished from this nation."

We have had four years of false prophecies, broken promises and blundering statesmanship.

Twelve years of reactionary policies have brought the nation to the worst crisis in its history; 11,000,000 idle laborers, 30,000,000 American people living on charity, 12,000 bank failures, thousands of idle factories, 600,000 home and farm foreclosures.

Agriculture is prostrate and on the verge of bankruptcy. Surplus food stuffs are smothering the farmer while millions of human beings are underfed or starving.

The President has proved his utter lack of capacity to restore the nation to economic health. The people have lost confidence in his leadership and will not be reassured by his baseless campaign forecasts of returning prosperity.

The battle has not been won! The fundamental cause of our distress has not been remedied! Each day of delay adds to human misery and despair!

THE NATION DEMANDS CONSTRUCTIVE LEADERSHIP!

ELECT . . . ROOSEVELT . . . *ELECT*

A campaign poster for Franklin Delano Roosevelt, 1932.
Franklin D. Roosevelt Presidential Library and Museum

Franklin Delano Roosevelt and Herbert Hoover on their way to the US Capitol for Roosevelt's inauguration, March 4, 1933. The nation's media were quick to pick up on the sharp contrast between the demeanors of each man.
Library of Congress, Prints and Photographs Division

since 1916. More people cast ballots for Roosevelt, nearly twenty-three million voters, than had ever voted for any presidential candidate in American history.

By the time Inauguration Day arrived, on March 4, 1933, Herbert Hoover was a bitter man. His policies had been roundly rejected by American voters, and his long career of service to the American people would be forever clouded by the Crash. Though they sat side by side, the president and president-elect of the United States of America didn't speak a single word to each other during their rain-soaked limousine ride from the White House to the Capitol steps. Hoover could barely contain his hatred for the new president, who beamed at the crowds gathered to watch the motorcade as it made its way toward the Capitol.

In the days and weeks that followed, the media, and all Americans, would see just how different a president FDR was destined to become.

Young people striking for higher wages at the King Farm in Morrisville, Pennsylvania, in August 1938.

John Vachon, photographer, Library of Congress, Farm Security Administration/Office of War Information Collection

PART TWO
RISE

I found a common understanding and unselfishness I'd never known. These people are real people and I'm glad I'm one of them. I only wish I'd got mad long ago and investigated, but I didn't have time for anything outside of my own small circle. I'm living for the first time with a definite goal. I want a decent living for not only my family but for everyone.

—VIOLET BAGGETT, A MEMBER OF THE WOMEN'S AUXILIARY SUPPORTING THE UNITED AUTOMOBILE WORKERS STRIKERS IN FLINT, MICHIGAN

Eleanor Roosevelt in 1933, the year her husband Franklin was sworn in as president of the United States—in the depths of the Great Depression.

CHAPTER THREE
IT TAKES TWO

The first week of FDR's presidency, more than 450,000 letters arrived at the White House, written by people sharing their gratitude, fears, and hopes with the new president. And the letters kept coming by the hundreds of thousands. Americans wrote him heartfelt personal notes; they sent telegrams; and they did not hesitate to stop him in the street when he was out in public. "I never saw him," one man remembered, "but I knew him. Can you have forgotten how, with his voice, he came into our house, the president of these United States, calling us friends?" FDR's portrait hung in living rooms across the country.

Franklin Delano Roosevelt had done more than win a landslide victory for the presidency. He now basked in the genuine affection of millions of Americans.

FDR's optimism was, among his many formidable strengths as a politician, the bedrock of his broad support. "A smile in the White House again seemed like a meal to us," the comedian Will Rogers quipped.

But Franklin Roosevelt also had a secret weapon, a force that would spearhead his new fight against the Great Depression.

Her name was Eleanor Roosevelt.

There had never been a First Lady like Eleanor Roosevelt. "Eleanor Roosevelt set a new pace, new goals, a new understanding of what was possible and acceptable for women to achieve," wrote her biographer Blanche Wiesen Cook. Nearly as popular as her husband, Eleanor arrived in Washington with goals, supporters, and power of her own. Letters addressed to "Dear Mrs. Roosevelt" piled up next to the president's, a testament to the hundreds of thousands (and eventually, millions) of women and girls who sought her advice and help. As she settled into the White House that winter, she did so not simply as Franklin's spouse but as his full political partner—a unique relationship that dated back nearly a quarter century.

Both the president and First Lady were born Roosevelts (fifth cousins, twice removed) in the early 1880s, members of the same extended and illustrious New York family. To be a Roosevelt was something close to royalty in nineteenth-century America. Roosevelts owned large manor houses overlooking the Hudson River and elegant town houses in New York City. They hunted foxes on horseback and attended lavish balls. FDR's family lived in a large estate in Hyde Park, New York, and traveled on their own private railroad car. Both Franklin and Eleanor were raised largely by governesses and educated as children by private tutors. (One of Franklin's childhood friends, noting the number of tutors he seemed to have, asked Franklin if he had a tutor for climbing trees.)

An only child with a strong-willed, domineering mother, FDR grew up wealthy and indulged. Pampered, spoiled, and aloof, he was nicknamed F.D.—for "feather duster"—by his classmates. His parents

Franklin Delano Roosevelt in 1893.
Franklin D. Roosevelt Presidential Library and Museum

groomed him to be a leader of the upper class; he attended private school at the exclusive Groton School, and continued his studies at Harvard University and then Columbia Law School. As a young man, Franklin loved to sail and to socialize. Nothing about his personality or modest accomplishments suggested the extraordinary life that lay ahead of him—let alone the possibility that he would become a hero to millions of regular, hard-working Americans.

Despite her equally impressive family tree, Eleanor's life was struck by hardship and challenges at an early age. Her parents, Anna and Elliott, were charming socialites who lived entirely off their considerable inheritances. (While Elliott's brother, Theodore Roosevelt, was building a political career, Elliott spent his years traveling, hunting, and shopping.) But their marriage was stormy and unpredictable, and Eleanor spent much of her childhood alone and starved for affection.

When she was six years old, her mother informed Eleanor coldly, "You have no looks, so see to it that you have manners." For the rest of her life, Eleanor would endure cruel judgments about her "looks." Even at a young age, she began to see the world differently and to sympathize with the limitations placed on women of all backgrounds.

Still, Eleanor idolized her father, Elliott, who returned her affections warmly—on the rare days he was at home. Elliott Roosevelt was a serious alcoholic, prone to depression and evidently incapable of controlling his destructive habits. One day, as he and Eleanor were walking their family dogs in New York City, he ducked into his favorite club for a brief moment while Eleanor was left to wait outside, holding the leashes. Six hours later, Eleanor was still waiting. Elliott, having passed out from too much to drink, was later carried out and deposited onto the sidewalk.

Eleanor was only eight years old when her mother died suddenly of diphtheria, a contagious and debilitating respiratory infection for which there was no cure—at least not until the discovery of antibiotics in the twentieth century. Two years later, in 1894, her father died from complications relating to alcoholism. An orphan at age ten, Eleanor was dependent on the generosity of aunts, uncles, and grandparents. She matured quickly, always alert to her own weaknesses and sympathetic to other people's vulnerabilities. "Very early," she wrote in her autobiography, "I became conscious of the fact that there were people around me who suffered in one way or another."

Eleanor and Franklin began their courtship when he was twenty and she nineteen. They were married in New York, in 1905, at a service attended by many of the nation's wealthiest families. Eleanor's uncle Teddy, now the president of the United States, took the train to New York from Washington to give the bride away.

Franklin and Eleanor in Hyde Park, New York, in 1906.
Franklin D. Roosevelt Presidential Library and Museum

In 1910, the Democratic Party unexpectedly invited Franklin to run for State Senate in New York. He leapt at the challenge. Having lived a life of complete and uninterrupted privilege, Franklin surprised everyone with his hardworking, easygoing manner and his natural ability to connect with regular people. But even more surprising was how politics transformed Eleanor, who proved herself a gifted organizer and networker among voters. With no real experience in work or politics, Eleanor soon became Franklin's most important strategist and adviser.

FDR's first election victory ignited his lifelong passion for electoral politics. Eleanor observed how "he took a satisfaction in the purely political side of the struggle, in achieving new office." After that first win, Franklin was never far from the political stage. Following two terms as state senator in New York, he served as assistant secretary of the Navy under President Woodrow Wilson, and then as candidate for vice president of the United States on the Democratic ticket with James M. Cox in 1920 (when they lost miserably to Republicans Warren G. Harding and Calvin Coolidge). A natural conversationalist with people from all backgrounds, Franklin would go on to make wildly popular public appearances, including a speech at the 1924 Democratic Convention that earned him an ovation that lasted over an hour.

As Franklin's political career soared, Eleanor gradually admitted to herself that her own future could not be a quiet, domestic one. But it took two painful experiences to finally persuade her to abandon the privacy of her household and carve out a public role of her own.

First, in September 1918, Eleanor discovered that Franklin had been involved in a love affair with her very own secretary, Lucy Mercer. She immediately proposed a divorce, but Franklin, knowing that a divorce could end his political career, broke off the relationship with Mercer and begged Eleanor's forgiveness. Their marriage recovered, but from that point onward, Eleanor resolved to set out on an independent path. "Life is meant to be lived," she declared. She threw herself into political and volunteer work, and she surrounded herself with a large network of intelligent, powerful, and politically active women—the first generation of American women to enter politics after winning the right to vote in 1920. She drove a car herself, and happily traveled alone, whether just into the city or across the country. With the help of her friend Amelia Earhart, the famous aviation pioneer, she even learned how to fly a plane, joining a small handful of early female aviators.

Barely two years later, a second shock finally propelled Eleanor into the public eye. During a trip to the Roosevelts' seaside home, Campobello, Franklin contracted polio, a painful and contagious disease that paralyzed his body from the waist down. It was a devastating setback for a man who cherished physical activity and who carefully polished his public image. Franklin spent the rest of his life in a wheelchair and could stand upright only with the help of heavy metal leg braces. He also made a point of keeping photographers and journalists away from his wheelchair, and despite his many years in public office, only a few pictures exist of him seated in it.

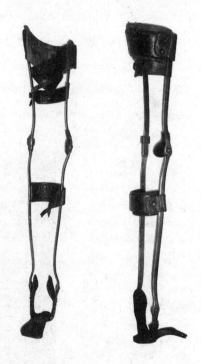

FDR's leg braces.
Franklin D. Roosevelt Presidential Library and Museum

Franklin's paralysis began a new chapter in Eleanor's life. From now on, Eleanor's physical mobility and her

independent spirit made her indispensable to the Roosevelt family—
and to Franklin's own career. She now served as his doppelgänger,
representing him at meetings and, after some practice and coach-
ing, giving speeches on his behalf. But Eleanor did not simply parrot
Franklin's views. She was convinced that the only way for people—
especially women—to improve the world was for them to gain political power. "Women must get into the political game," she argued,
"and stay in it." By the mid-1920s, Eleanor had waded up to her chin
into New York politics.

A key figure in the League of Women Voters and the Women's
Division of the New York State Democratic Committee, Eleanor Roosevelt had made herself one of the most recognizable and influential
people in New York State. She championed causes that improved
the lives of working women, including the forty-eight-hour, five-day
workweek—at a time when unsafe workplaces were common, and

Members of the
League of Women
Voters meet at Eleanor
Roosevelt's home in
Hyde Park, New York, in
the 1920s. During the
1920s, she was widely
considered one of the
most important political
leaders in New York
State—even though
she herself did not hold
public office.
Division of Rare and Manuscript
Collections, Cornell University

all workers were required to stay on the job for six days a week, ten hours a day. She advocated for unemployment insurance, to help support workers who had lost their jobs through no fault of their own. She fought to make sure that children had safe food and water, good schools, and playgrounds, and were not allowed to hold adult jobs. Eleanor believed that although men still controlled the levers of political power, women were the ones who saw what needed fixing in society—and understood how to do it.

In 1928, the Democratic Party again tapped Franklin, without warning, to run for political office—this time for governor of New York State. In a year when Democrats took a beating nationally, FDR won the governor's race by a slim margin of votes, a victory that helped make

Franklin Roosevelt in New York in 1929, displaying the smile that helped win him millions of admirers.
Franklin D. Roosevelt Presidential Library and Museum

him the Democratic Party's new star. Roosevelt's growing crowd of admirers attributed his success to his sunny outlook, his oratorical skills, and his progressive, forward-looking bent. He once summed up his approach to leadership in this way: "It is common sense to take a method and try it: If it fails, admit it frankly and try another. But above all, try something."

Eleanor's star rose alongside Franklin's. On the surface, she was now the First Lady of New York, the governor's wife. Behind the scenes, she was a woman with her own strong opinions about how America needed to change, and with the political power to accomplish her goals. The Roosevelt team had taken shape. Franklin was the politician, the man who inspired voters and won elections; Eleanor had the solutions, and the relationships, to get things done.

Four years later, when FDR was elected president of the United States, Eleanor joined him in Washington as a force in her own right—a national sensation even before she first walked through the front doors of her new home, the White House. With FDR's encouragement, Eleanor assembled her own team of allies and advisers and worked alongside her husband as a fierce advocate for a new idea of what America could be.

Eleanor used her position to call attention to the plight of those suffering most during the Depression—their "eyes and ears," she said. She wrote regularly—sometimes

Dear Mrs. Roosevelt,

I was so thrilled on listening to your two talks Tuesday night that I have girded up my courage in order to write you to express my great appreciation. What a blessing it is for me, a shut in—at the age of 84 to listen to the voice of the most remarkable woman, who to my knowledge ever occupied the White House.

Very Respectfully,

Marie C. Hurley
Washington, DC

daily—for major magazines, developing a large and devoted reader-
ship. (When she asked readers to "Write to Me," more than three
hundred thousand people sent letters to the White House.) Once a
week, Eleanor Roosevelt held her own press conferences, which she
limited to women reporters only—because she knew the challenges
they faced, and wanted to give them special access to the White
House. She also made more than three hundred radio broadcasts
while FDR was president, including one on NBC Radio, titled *Mrs.
Eleanor Roosevelt's Own Program.* She was one of the nation's top

Eleanor Roosevelt's first press conference at the White House in 1933, a landmark
event for women journalists in the United States.
Franklin D. Roosevelt Presidential Library and Museum

radio professionals, so popular that she earned $3,000 for
each appearance (nearly
$50,000 in today's dollars)
and connected regularly with
an audience of many millions
of Americans.

Like FDR, Eleanor quickly
earned a reputation for
warmth and approachability.
She frequently traveled alone,
and rejected Secret Service
or police protection. In May
1933, when three thousand

Eleanor Roosevelt speaking with the press
in Los Angeles, California, on June 6, 1933.
Franklin D. Roosevelt Presidential Library and Museum

veterans returned to Washington to lobby the government once again
for the bonus that was owed to them, Eleanor drove out to their camp
in Fort Hood, Virginia, accompanied only by her close friend and
White House aide Lewis Howe. (Howe slept in the car while she met
with the men alone to listen to their concerns.) Barely a year after
their violent eviction from the nation's capital, the veterans were wary
of Roosevelt's promises of help. But by the end of the meeting, she had
won them over. "There was no kind of disturbance," she reported later
to the press, "[and] nothing but the most courteous behavior."

Similar episodes became one of the hallmarks of the new First
Lady's relationships with ordinary Americans. Often behind the
wheel of her own car, Eleanor toured the country constantly, giving

lectures and lending support to many different causes, and (as she had done when her husband was governor) reporting back what she had learned. During one three-month period, she traveled more than forty thousand miles.

Eleanor Roosevelt eats a "Five Cent Meal" at a conference of Daughters of the Great Depression. The cost of the meal was based on the average food budget of American families at that time.
Harris & Ewing, photographer, Library of Congress, Prints and Photographs Division

As president and First Lady, Franklin and Eleanor Roosevelt were not only husband and wife, but also each other's closest confidant and most reliable political ally. Like Franklin, Eleanor kept up a gigantic network of friends, supporters, readers, and informal advisers. Above all, she helped mobilize those people who had previously found themselves excluded from American politics—especially women—and made sure the White House stayed sympathetic to their needs and hopes.

It was almost as if America now had two presidents, each one ready to tackle the biggest challenge the country ever faced. And it wasn't long before the Roosevelts set their plans for a new America into motion.

CHAPTER FOUR
PUSHING BACK

Rain clouds hung over the nation's capital on Inauguration Day in March 1933. When Franklin Delano Roosevelt arrived at the stage in front of the US Capitol, his son had to help him climb the steps to the podium. He was the first and, to date, the only US president with a major disability, at a time when few disabled people had any role in public or professional life. What he called his "good cheer"—in the face of incredible pain and physical challenges— would become part of the new energy he wished to inject into America.

Following his swearing-in as president, FDR stepped forward to address the nation. His ringing words, broadcast

The New Deal, a mural by Conrad Albrizio dedicated to President Roosevelt (and featuring his image, standing in the center), placed in the auditorium of the Leonardo da Vinci Art School, at 149 East Thirty-Fourth Street in New York City.
Franklin D. Roosevelt Presidential Library and Museum

on every radio station and printed in every newspaper, instantly cut through the sense of doom looming over the country.

> This is preeminently the time to speak the truth, the whole truth, frankly and boldly. Nor need we shrink from honestly facing conditions in our country today. This great nation will endure as it has endured, will revive and will prosper. So first of all let me assert my firm belief that **the only thing we have to fear is fear itself,** [emphasis added]—nameless, unreasoning, unjustified terror which paralyzes needed efforts to convert retreat into advance. In every dark hour of our national life a leadership of frankness and vigor has met with that understanding and support of the people themselves which is essential to victory.

The Hollywood actress Lillian Gish remarked that FDR "seemed to have been dipped in phosphorus," because his words shone through the foul weather. A schoolteacher from North Carolina named Sarah Love was in the audience that day. She turned to a man standing beside her and commented, "Any man who can talk like that in times like these is worthy of every ounce of support a true American has."

In the final moments of his speech, FDR called for "action, and action now"—and he soon showed that he meant it.

The original copy of Roosevelt's inaugural address, with his handwritten notes. His words "the only thing we have to fear is fear itself" have gone down in history as one of the most powerful and memorable phrases ever spoken by a president.

Franklin D. Roosevelt Presidential Library and Museum

The day after his inauguration, Roosevelt declared a *national* bank holiday, ordering all banks throughout the United States to close—to prevent any more money from being withdrawn. He then called Congress into a special session, and by the end of the week, the Emergency Banking Relief Act was signed into law, directing financial support to all banks when they reopened the following Monday. Things moved so quickly that there was not enough time to print copies of the bill for members of Congress to read. Most voted on it without having glanced at a single word.

On Sunday, March 12, at ten o'clock, the night before the banks reopened, Roosevelt spoke to the nation in the first of thirty national radio broadcasts over the course of his presidency. These were dubbed "fireside chats" by the media because of their intimate, informal quality, not unlike opinions shared by a family member in the warmth of a living room. No president had ever spoken to Americans on so personal a level.

Sixty million people—almost half of the country—gathered around their radios to listen to Roosevelt.

In a reassuring, upbeat tone, the president carefully explained the new banking law and told Americans that "it is safer to keep your money in a reopened bank than under the mattress." He encouraged Americans to have faith in his plans. "We have provided the machinery to restore our financial system," he told them, "it is up to you to support and make it work."

A father and daughter in California tune in to one of Roosevelt's radio addresses, 1930s.
National Archives and Records Administration

It is your problem no less than it is mine. Together we cannot fail.

—FRANKLIN DELANO ROOSEVELT, FIRST FIRESIDE CHAT,

MARCH 12, 1933

The next day, people all over the country formed long lines at banks—to put their money back in. By the end of that week, Americans returned $600 million into their accounts. Within two weeks, $1 billion had been deposited into American banks.

WESTERN UNION

Received at 708 14th St., N. W., Washington, D. C.

JA450 62 DL=COLUMBUS IND 13 955A

PRESIDENT FRANKLIN D ROOSEVELT=

WASHDC=

AS THE SMALL TOWN HARD SHELLED REPUBLICANS OF THE MIDDLE
WEST WHO WORKED AGAINST AND VOTED AGAINST ALL DEMOCRATS I
WANT TO ANNOUNCE THAT I JOIN WITH MILLIONS OF OTHER COMMON
FOLKS OUT THIS WAY WHO HAVE BEEN WON OVER TO COMPLETE
CONFIDENCE IN OUR NEW PRESIDENT AND HIS METHOD OF GETTING
THINGS DONE THAT SPEECH LAST NIGHT WAS A SOUL THRILLER=

FRANK H SPARKS.

Dear President;

I would like to tell you that I enjoyed
the speech which you have just finished
giving. I have regained faith in the banks
due to your earnest beliefs. I had decided
that, as soon as the banks in Minneapolis
reopened, I would withdraw my money. When
you said that people's money would be safer
in the banks than under their mattresses
I decided I'd leave my money just where
it is.

Although I'm only a high school
student I take a great interest in the
country's problems. I firmly believe that
the country is on the upward grade
and I believe that if people will remain
calm and composed that the government
will pull the United States out of this
terrible depression.

I should like you to know that
the Monday following your inauguration,
our entire French class sent up prayers
to God for your safety and protection.

If you could possibly find a
moment's time during your busy days
would you please write a note back
to me and acknowledge my letter?

"God be with you and bless
you," dear President.

Very respectfully yours,
Viola Hazelberger

Notes to President Roosevelt.
Franklin D. Roosevelt Presidential Library and Museum

In one bold stroke, Roosevelt had beaten back the worst of the banking emergency.

Roosevelt believed that the American government was the only force powerful enough to jump-start the economy and push back against the Depression. America was ready for what FDR called a "New Deal."

Now was the time to show what government could do. From March to June 1933, Roosevelt's New Deal attacked the Great Depression with an arsenal of programs, projects, and experiments devised by a group of experts who came to be known as the "Brain Trust." The White House bustled with new faces. Spurred on by FDR, more new laws were passed in the spring of 1933 than at any session of Congress before or since. One historian called these hundred days "the third great revolution in American history"—as significant as the American Revolution and the Civil War.

Before the New Deal, the government mostly left Americans to fend for themselves. Now, as Madelyn Davidson of Montpelier, Vermont, remembered, "everybody was helping everybody." Roosevelt's New Dealers appeared everywhere, setting up job programs, building bridges, handing out food, and giving people a sense that better times were on the way.

The New Deal's first big steps helped calm the sense of panic that had seized America in the early 1930s. But FDR knew that many Americans were still teetering on the edge of hopelessness, and that time was running out. "Our greatest task is to put people to work," FDR said.

James Franco of San Diego was one of those people. For two years after his father's fish market went out of business, James and his family had worked off and on at odd jobs—anything to keep the bills paid. Once, after inquiring at every restaurant downtown, James found an opening as a dishwasher. "Ten dollars a week, twelve hours a day," he recalled. "If he had said fourteen hours a day I would have said gladly—I remember how I ran most of the way home, I was so eager to tell my parents the happy news."

James's happy news soured after only one month on the job. "Jim," his boss informed him, "I don't know how to tell you, but I have to hire a man who has five small children. He doesn't even expect any money. All he wants is just enough food to take home to his family at night." Once again, Franco was out of work.

What saved James Franco and his family in the spring of 1933 was a new program called the Civilian Conservation Corps, or the CCC. The nation's first job program for young people, the CCC provided young men with shelter, food, and paid work.

The CCC paid each man

A recruitment poster for the CCC in Illinois, 1933.
Federal Art Project, Work Projects Administration Poster Collection, Library of Congress

$30 per month (an amount equal to around $550 today), and required him to send $25 home to his family. "I found myself with a job—as long as I wanted it," Franco said. "Thirty dollars a month, twenty-five went to the family and a whole five dollar bill went to me. That was big money back then."

If Americans had any doubts that FDR planned to move fast against the Depression, then they were put to rest by the CCC. From the middle of May until early July 1933, the CCC enrolled 9,000 young men per day into its ranks. That summer, more than 350,000 people began work at CCC camps all over the United States. According to Robert Fechner, the CCC's first director, "it was the most rapid large-scale mobilization of men the country had ever witnessed."

In just two years, the CCC built 2,650 camps, in every state across the country. Each one of these camps housed up to two hundred men, who slept in barracks, ate in mess halls, and relaxed in recreation centers. New recruits were fed heartily and given free medical care, and the CCC handed out clothing, books, toothbrushes, and even new shoes.

A CCC mess hall in the Black Hills of South Dakota, July 1933. The men built the camp structures themselves.
National Archives and Records Administration

Carroll Burnette of Florida, along with his brother, joined the "three Cs" as a teenager, and worked in Florida and California for the rest of the decade. "If it had not been for the CCC, I don't know how [we] would have survived. It was a humanitarian program. We were rescued."

Throughout the Great Depression, men turned to the CCC for jobs, food, and shelter. Between 1933 and 1942, two and a half million men signed up for the Corps.

The CCC alone did not end the Depression. But this and other New Deal programs sent a signal to struggling people that the government aimed to play a new role in their lives.

As months went by, FDR and his Brain Trust launched what came to be known as "alphabet soup" agencies

CCC workers constructing a road in 1933. Through long days and hard labor, CCC workers planted three billion trees and built eight hundred parks.
National Archives and Records Administration, Franklin D. Roosevelt Library Public Domain Photographs

(named for the sheer number of initials used to identify them): the Public Works Administration (PWA), the Federal Emergency Relief Administration (FERA), the Civil Works Administration (CWA), the Agricultural Adjustment Administration (AAA), the Works Progress Administration (WPA), the Tennessee Valley Authority (TVA), and many others. Each of these brought the full power of the US government into communities all over the country, offering jobs, money, and hope.

B. C. Aaron's ramshackle rented cabin, before he received help from the New Deal. To solve the housing crisis, the Homeowners Refinancing Act offered financial support to people at risk of losing their homes to foreclosure. Between 1933 and 1935, the program saved more than a million homes. Other New Deal programs helped build new homes for people who could not afford them.
Library of Congress, Farm Security Administration/ Office of War Information Collection, 1939

B. C. Aaron's new house, purchased with a New Deal loan.
Library of Congress, Farm Security Administration/ Office of War Information Collection, 1939

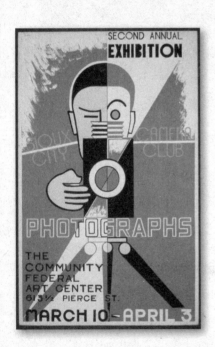

This WPA poster advertises a photography exhibit in Sioux City, Iowa. Artists created more than two thousand WPA posters during the Great Depression; they hung in shop windows, bus stations, libraries, and schools across the country, adding a dash of color to drab streets and communicating important information about New Deal programs.
Federal Art Project, Work Projects Administration Poster Collection, Library of Congress

A New Mexico farmer and a government representative review the AAA program to determine how it could be applied on that farm, in 1934. To the millions of people who still lived in rural areas and farmed the land, the AAA paid farmers cash in exchange for reducing the amount of crops they grew. The theory, which proved correct, was that a reduced supply of crops would increase prices and help farmers get back on their feet.

National Archives and Records Administration

A dam built by the WPA in Egg Harbor, New Jersey, in 1936. For the millions of Americans who could not find work as the Depression lingered into 1934 and beyond, FDR created the Works Progress Administration, or the WPA. During its eight-year life—from 1935 to 1943—the WPA employed nearly nine million people, who built bridges, schools, and parks in every corner of the United States. President Roosevelt's biggest experiment turned out to be the largest single employer in the country.

Historic American Engineering Record Collection, Prints and Photographs Division, Library of Congress

TVA workmen assembling a giant electrical generator on the Norris Dam in Tennessee in the mid-1930s. The TVA built huge dams and hydroelectric facilities across a sprawling, impoverished region that included Tennessee, Georgia, Mississippi, Kentucky, North Carolina, and Virginia. The organization created thousands of new jobs, and also generated low-cost electricity for millions of customers in the region. It was one of the largest construction projects in history.

Library of Congress, Farm Security Administration/Office of War Information Collection

A school built by the WPA in Franklin, Georgia, one of thousands built all over the country. Many are still in operation.

Jack Delano, photographer, Library of Congress, Farm Security Administration/Office of War Information Collection, 1941

One small mining town in Alabama, named Carbon Hill, learned firsthand about what the New Deal could do.

Miners from the Chickasaw Mine, in Carbon Hill, Alabama, 1930s.
Photographic Section, Division of Information Service, WPA, National Archives and Records Administration

In 1931, the Crash nearly flattened Carbon Hill. When the local Chickasaw coal mine closed that year, three-quarters of the town's population lost their jobs. There were two banks in Carbon Hill, and both of them failed. As the town's tax revenues dried up, schools, sidewalks, and buildings fell into disrepair. Roads turned to mud when it rained. With no functioning sewer system and abandoned mine pits near the town, pools of filthy water collected and bred mosquitoes. Outbreaks of malaria (a flulike disease carried by mosquitoes) were common among the poor and unemployed. According to a government report, Carbon Hill was "on absolute economic bottom." Maude Patterson, a local beauty shop owner, described her home as "one of the poorest towns in the county, and one of the poorest counties in the state."

Two years later, following FDR's election, nearly a half dozen New Deal programs started rolling into town.

First, the CWA helped repair Carbon Hill's grammar school, its city hall, and the town garage. Then PWA funds went toward building a new high school and a new sewer system. Later, the WPA constructed a new swimming pool and recreational center—as well as a new jail. The WPA also repaired the town's crumbling sidewalks, gutters, and streets (only one of which had been paved before the Depression), changes that "improved our town more than any other one thing," according to H. E. Baker, the local pharmacist.

Most important, local people from Carbon Hill performed all this work. The town's postmaster, Albert Shaw, reported that out of a population of 2,500 people, "nearly one in every five" received paychecks from the WPA. "They are distributed from this office every two weeks," he said, adding that "our WPA Payroll means about as much as our local industrial payroll."

George Gilder, a doctor in Carbon Hill, believed that the government programs "saved the lives of lots of people, or kept them from going hungry at least." A local laborer, Ben Pair, put it simply: "If they hadn't had WPA people would've just gone down to the stores and taken what they needed. When the kids look an' say, 'Daddy, I'm hungry,' why—you just got to have food."

"Some turn up their noses but if it hadn't been for the WPA the doors of half the stores'd been closed. Sidewalks make it easier to keep the house clean. Curbs and gutters keep the streets from washing out. Roosevelt has been a wonderful, wonderful president." —Mrs. Aileen Brown, pictured in a store in Carbon Hill, 1930s.
Photographic Section, Division of Information Service, WPA, National Archives and Records Administration

Thousands of communities, in every county in the United States, welcomed the relief brought by the New Deal. Roosevelt, with his infectious optimism, had aimed the nation "on the upward grade." After so much suffering, it seemed that things might be getting better. In the spring of 1933, as temperatures warmed, few Americans could escape the feeling that something else had thawed out as well: hope for a better future.

An elderly woman living in a homeless camp near Bakersfield, California. She remarked to the photographer, "If you lose your pluck you lose the most there is in you—all you've got to live with."

Dorothea Lange, photographer, Library of Congress, Farm Security Administration/Office of War Information Collection, 1936

CHAPTER FIVE
THE REVOLUTIONARY

As the first term of his presidency unfolded, Franklin Roosevelt could feel that the county's mood was shifting. Hundreds of thousands of people were lining up for new jobs. The threat of widespread starvation and the other immediate dangers seemed to have receded. The New Deal was up and running. And yet the thousands upon thousands of letters arriving at the White House seemed to tell a bigger, more troubling story about the real America—one that had remained hidden from the nation's political leaders until then. One-third of all Americans, including almost every person over the age of sixty-five, earned barely enough money to survive *before* the Crash. After the Crash, that percentage had increased to well over half of the entire American population.

Americans were hardworking and resourceful, but most of them were also very, very poor. The Great Depression, the president discovered, didn't *create* poverty in the United States—it simply

> *I am now 72 years old and have never had anything. I have always been poor, and have always worked hard, so now I am not able to do any more. I am all worn out but am able to be around and I thank God that I have no pains. It is hard to be old and not have anything. I do not own as much as one cent to my name, so I know God would bless you, if you could help us to get more money for pension, so we would have enough to eat.*
>
> —MRS. A.A., PETERSBURG, NORTH DAKOTA, MARCH 21, 1934

spread poverty to the majority of Americans. The problem, in short, was even bigger and more deeply rooted than most people in Washington had realized.

Older people were especially vulnerable. In 1933, only 5 percent of elderly people had a pension, or a regular source of money to support them in their retirement. The rest depended on a rickety system of meager handouts and the kindness of relatives, and the least fortunate ended up at poorhouses (sometimes called "almshouses"). Poorhouses have been long since forgotten, but they dotted America's countryside, towns, and cities well into the 1930s. They were usually miserable, cold, and crowded. Supported mostly by charitable donations and some local taxes, a poorhouse was the last stop for the destitute, the mentally ill, and the elderly.

In 1933, close to seven million elderly people lacked adequate help, money, or shelter. America needed a more permanent fix, something to ease the suffering of so many millions of citizens and also keep the *next* generation from falling into the same poverty trap. It

The women's dormitory of the Kings County Almshouse, New York City, in 1900.
Museum of the City of New York

turned out that FDR had just the person in mind to take on such a challenge—an unlikely hero, for these most unusual times.

Frances Perkins's eyes were opened to the reality of poverty in 1898, as a student at Mount Holyoke College in Massachusetts— one of the few colleges for women in the nineteenth century. At that time, many middle- and upper-class Americans assumed that people were poor because of laziness, stupidity, or alcoholism. But Professor Annah May Soule taught her students differently. Soule made them spend time in local textile mills, to observe and write about the struggles of regular working people. Perkins's experiences in Soule's classroom forever changed her view of the world.

Soon afterward, Perkins came across a book of photographs by the documentary photographer Jacob Riis, titled *How the Other Half Lives*. Riis's book portrayed the lives of desperately poor immigrants, including many young children, scraping by in hidden corners of New York, America's largest, most prosperous city. Riis's work shook Perkins to her core.

After graduating from Mount Holyoke, Perkins moved to Chicago and joined up with Hull House, the pioneering "settlement house" founded by Jane Addams. Located in an Italian immigrant slum on the South Side of the city, Hull House provided housing, food, medical

Frances Perkins in 1915, wearing her trademark headgear. By accident or design, her hats resembled those worn by soldiers in the American Revolution.
Bain Collection, Library of Congress Prints and Photographs Division

care, education, and citizenship classes for Chicago's neediest immi-grant families. It also built the city's first public playground and gym-nasium. Addams's work in Chicago sparked a national movement that eventually led to the building of over five hundred settlement houses nationwide and inspired thousands of young activists to join the fight to improve society.

As she distributed food and milk to hungry children and learned about their parents' long working hours and low wages, Frances questioned how America was supposed to function without ade-quate support for its working people. Led by Jane Addams's example, she had found her calling. Perkins committed herself to a career of working on behalf of the poor and unemployed; "I had to do some-thing about unnecessary hazards to life, unnecessary poverty," she recalled. "It was sort of up to me."

Just a few years later, Frances enrolled at the School of Social Work at Columbia University in New York City. She also took a job with the New York Consumers League, an organization devoted to protect-ing the workers who made American consumer goods. Though still a young woman, Frances rose quickly through its ranks to become executive secretary, in 1910.

On March 25, 1911, Frances was sitting down for tea in an elegant apartment overlooking Washington Square Park in Manhattan. Sud-denly, a butler interrupted with the news that smoke was billowing out of a tall building just a block away. A fiery blaze had broken out at the Triangle Shirtwaist Factory. The garment manufacturer employed hundreds of young men and women, many of them recent immigrants from Italy, Russia, and Poland. They worked elbow to elbow at long tables on the upper floors of the tall building, piecing together shirts and blouses through grueling twelve-hour work shifts.

Frances had to lift up her skirts to run the short distance across Washington Square Park. A terrible scene unfolded before her.

William Shepherd, a reporter and eyewitness to the fire, phoned in the details to his newspaper in Milwaukee:

> I was walking through Washington Square when a puff of smoke issuing from the factory building caught my eye. I reached the building before the alarm was turned in. I saw every feature of the tragedy visible from outside the building. I learned a new sound—a more horrible sound than description can picture. It was the thud of a speeding, living body on a stone sidewalk.
>
> Thud-dead, thud-dead, thud-dead, thud-dead. Sixty-two thud-deads. I call them that, because the sound and the thought of death came to me each time, at the same instant. There was plenty of chance to watch them as they came down. The height was eighty feet.

Shepherd's real-time reporting, along with dozens of other first-person accounts, shocked the nation. The entire building, they

Firefighters battle the Triangle Shirtwaist Factory fire in New York City in 1911.

revealed, was a firetrap. Only a handful of safety precautions had been taken, and none of them worked. The Triangle Shirtwaist Factory was an accident waiting to happen—and it was no different from thousands of other workplaces across the nation.

One hundred forty-six people, most of them young women—many of whom jumped to their death—perished in the Triangle Shirtwaist Factory fire.

Frances Perkins would never forget what she had seen: "I can't begin to tell you how disturbed the people were everywhere. It was as though we had all done something wrong." The fire, she realized, was not just an

The broken fire escape at the Triangle Shirtwaist Factory, which prevented workers from escaping.
Franklin D. Roosevelt Presidential Library and Museum

accident or a simple tragedy. It was a failure on the part of America to protect its own citizens. Until that day, Frances had believed that private efforts such as Hull House or the New York Consumers League held the key to reforming America's cities and factories. But the fire convinced her that *government* was the only force big enough to protect ordinary Americans from this kind of tragedy. From that moment on, Frances quietly vowed to start a movement to change how government looked after all Americans. March 25,

1911, Perkins would say, was the day "the New Deal began" for her.

Perkins made herself into the nation's leading expert on fire safety, working conditions in factories, wages and working hours, and child labor. She led brave investigations—sometimes taking politicians on unannounced tours of dangerous factories—and lobbied for new laws to increase what people were paid and to limit the number of hours they worked.

Perkins had to play her role on a stage almost completely controlled by the opposite sex. It was not until 1920 that the women's suffrage movement succeeded in winning the right to vote for women, with the passage of the Nineteenth Amendment in 1919. Few if any women held positions of political power. Perkins knew that she had to play her role carefully, and became an expert at observing and understanding men. She saved her notes in a red envelope labeled "Notes on the Male Mind."

In just one example, Perkins observed early on that men "know and respect their mothers—ninety-nine percent of them do." So she intentionally started dressing in a plain, matronly style, which was calculated to gain the confidence of her male colleagues.

And it seemed to work. As a trusted confidante to New York State governor Alfred E. Smith, and then his successor, Governor Franklin Delano Roosevelt, Perkins learned everything she could about the lives of working people, and about what the government could do to make them safer and more secure. During the 1920s—when most political leaders tried to make the government do *less*—Perkins knew exactly how to pull the levers of power to make government do *more*.

When the nation faced the greatest crisis in its history, no American was more ready to come up with solutions. Rumors had been circulating that Perkins might be appointed to a senior position in the White House, and when Perkins was summoned to meet with FDR, she had an inkling of what was in store. Roosevelt came right to the point: "I've been thinking things over and I've decided I want you to be secretary of labor."

The president-elect was aware that appointing a woman to such an important government post would be controversial. Letters and telegrams for and against Perkins's appointment had been streaming into his office for weeks.

FOR

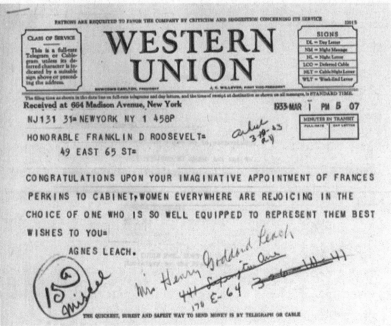

Franklin D. Roosevelt Presidential Library and Museum

As the first female nominee for cabinet secretary in US history, Frances Perkins had maneuvered her way into the world's most powerful and exclusive men's club. No woman had ever held such an

AGAINST

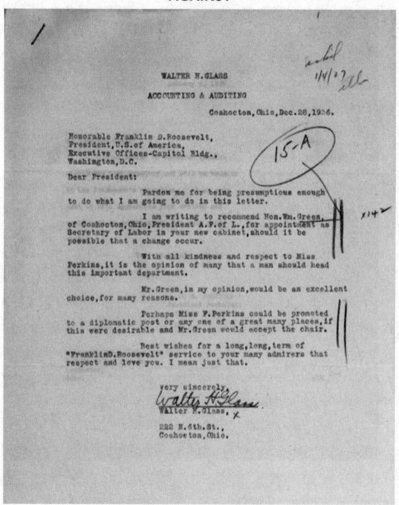

Franklin D. Roosevelt Presidential Library and Museum

influential official position in the US government. She later recalled that "I said that if I accepted the position of Secretary of Labor I should want to do a great deal...[and I] received Roosevelt's hearty endorsement, and he told me he wanted me to carry it out....And so I agreed to become Secretary of Labor after a conversation that lasted but an hour."

Perkins got the job.

Barely a year later, in 1934, FDR handed Perkins the biggest assignment of her career: He wanted her to design and build America's first social safety net. "You care about this thing," Roosevelt said to her. "You believe in it. Therefore, I know you will put your back to it more than anyone else, and you will drive it through."

There was no time to lose. Outside of the nation's capital, a growing chorus of voices was calling for much more radical change. Americans crowded into meeting halls and circus tents to hear about new schemes for creating a national retirement plan. The most popular of these was hatched by a modest sixty-five-year-old doctor named Francis Townsend. The "Townsend Plan" called for the federal government to give a $200-per-month pension to *every person* over the age of sixty. Townsend's followers gathered *twenty million signatures* from Americans, demanding that his plan be adopted by Congress.

If adopted, economists believed, the Townsend Plan would have quickly bankrupted the Federal Treasury. But neither the Townsend Plan nor other proposals being touted in 1934 stood a realistic chance of gaining Congress's approval—or surviving the Supreme Court's scrutiny.

A Townsend Plan supporter in Columbus, Kansas.

Arthur Rothstein, photographer, Library of Congress, Farm Security Administration/Office of War Information Collection, 1936

Perkins toiled away for months, and emerged just after Christmas with a plan called "Social Security." It would be the biggest single program ever launched by the US government, and a preemptive strike against any future depression.

The Social Security Act was signed into law on August 14, 1935. Frances Perkins—the only woman present—stood at the president's side during the signing ceremony. New York World-Telegram and the Sun Newspaper Photograph Collection, Library of Congress, Prints and Photographs Division

For the first time, America made a promise that *everyone* would be spared the worst effects of poverty, old age, and unemployment. The Social Security Act wove together the first three strands of a safety net that still protects Americans today:

- Help for spouses and children when a worker was killed or injured.
- A monthly check sent to retired workers for the rest of their lives.
- Unemployment insurance, providing protection when a worker lost a job.

 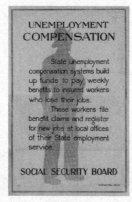 

Social Security Administration posters, 1936–39.
Social Security Administration

In the beginning, many people were excluded from the protections that Social Security offered. Despite Frances Perkins's efforts, the Social Security Act did not cover domestic workers (such as maids) or farm laborers, and this meant that 65 percent of African Americans were denied the benefits of Social Security. One African American civil rights leader called the Social Security Act "a sieve with holes just big enough for the majority of Negroes to fall through." Not

We can never insure one hundred percent of the population against one hundred percent of the hazards and vicissitudes of life, but we have tried to frame a law which will give some measure of protection to the average citizen and to his family against the loss of a job and against poverty-ridden old age.

—FDR'S STATEMENT ON SIGNING THE
SOCIAL SECURITY ACT

until the 1950s, almost twenty years later, was the law changed to cover all working Americans.

In 1936, the new Social Security office in the Candler Building in Baltimore hummed with the clicking of machines and the sorting of paper forms.

Workers at the Social Security headquarters in Baltimore, Maryland, in 1937, enter numbers into keypunch machines, giving each person a unique record.
Harris & Ewing, photographer, Library of Congress, Prints and Photographs Division

People all over the United States mailed in applications to receive a freshly printed Social Security card, and huge brown sacks of mail began to pile up. Government employees faced the monumental task of creating a system that could keep track of the names, addresses, ages, and monthly earnings of approximately thirty million people.

The first person to receive a monthly Social Security check—for $22.54—was Ida May Fuller of Ludlow, Vermont. Although

An unemployed lumber worker in Oregon with his wife. His Social Security number is tattooed on his arm.

Dorothea Lange, photographer, Library of Congress, Farm Security Administration/Office of War Information Collection, 1939

she retired in 1939 at the age of sixty-five, Fuller lived to be one hundred years old, and died in 1974. In the decades in between, the payments increased, both for Ida May Fuller and every working person in the country. Today, more than fifty million Americans receive monthly retirement checks through Social Security.

I come from an old American family who pioneered this country—They did not build this country so that their posterity should starve in it. **I believe that this country owes a living to every man, woman, and child. If it can't give us this living thru private industry it** *must* **provide for us through government means** [emphasis added]*—I am ready to fight for what I believe to be an inalienable right of every person living under this government.*

—A.B. [LETTER FROM A PRIVATE CITIZEN TO HARRY HOPKINS, ONE OF FDR'S CLOSEST NEW DEAL ADVISERS]

Ida May Fuller, the first Social Security recipient, 1939.
Social Security Administration

FDR had shown Americans that they could expect more from their government—that being a free citizen included the right to be secure from the threat of starvation, unemployment, and homelessness. With few exceptions, Americans agreed with him.

Many people were now ready to fight for that new kind of freedom. The Roosevelts and their Brain Trust in Washington could craft a New Deal, but they could not build a new world alone. To succeed, they needed allies.

CHAPTER SIX
A NEW WORLD

The men and women who worked hardest to pull America out of the Great Depression were accustomed to hard labor. Flattened by the Crash, America's working people—its factory workers, miners, farmers, seamstresses, lumberjacks, longshoremen, and others—had the most to gain from a new way of thinking about what it meant to be a citizen.

In the early years of the Depression, jobs could be dirty, dangerous, exhausting—and unreliable. A typical factory worker in New Jersey recalled what life was like on the job, for those lucky to be employed at all: "It was a ten-hour workday. You worked Saturdays. And if you had to work on holidays, you had no choice. They didn't like you, they fired you." An autoworker in Detroit, Russell Gage, described how the breakneck pace of the assembly line could mean that even a drink of water was out of the question. "That water fountain wasn't over ten feet from me," he said. "I worked for an hour and I wanted a drink of water and I didn't have time to get it." But the main issue for workers was not simply how much they earned or

Workers welding Buick fenders on an assembly line in Flint, Michigan, in 1935.

how long they worked: it was how much control they had over their lives, on the job. In the early 1930s, that question had been answered in favor of the boss. "We couldn't call our souls our own," commented one steelworker in Aliquippa, Pennsylvania.

Years of hard work, low pay, and long hours caused workers' complaints to pile up. Some of the worst grievances came from those who toiled deep underground. Coal had been mined for decades all across Pennsylvania, West Virginia, Ohio, Illinois, Indiana, and Iowa, where mine owners treated coal-mining towns as their private kingdoms. As one West Virginia miner summed things up: "We work in *his* mine. We live in *his* house. Our children go to *his* school. On Sunday we're preached at by *his* preacher. When we die we're buried in *his* cemetery."

Coal miners in Williamson, West Virginia, in 1935, resting with their lunch buckets before descending deep into the mine, where they would dig coal for twelve hours or more.
Ben Shahn, photographer, Library of Congress, Farm Security Administration/Office of War Information Collection

A typical coal miner's shack in West Virginia, with no indoor plumbing or electricity.
Marion Post Wolcott, photographer, Library of Congress, Farm Security Administration/Office of War Information Collection, 1938

The son of Welsh immi-
grants, John L. Lewis went to
work in Lucas, Iowa, when he
was eleven years old. At that
young age, Lewis lived a life
of risk and danger, breathing
in coal dust, tending mules
underground, and duck-
ing carefully when explosive
charges were set deep in the
mine shafts.

Lewis had ambitions
beyond the mines, how-
ever. Even as a young man,
he discovered that his voice
attracted attention. He learned
to tune it carefully during
his years with an amateur
opera company in Iowa, and
he could project it without

In the early years of the twentieth
century, the photographer Lewis Hine
captured images of child laborers all
over the United States. According to
Hine's notes, "This young [mule] driver
has been working...every day for a year."
The boy is wearing a miner's lamp to
illuminate the pitch-dark mine shafts
where he works.
Lewis W. Hine, photographer, The Miriam and Ira
D. Wallach Division of Art, Prints and Photographs:
Photography Collection, New York Public Library

amplification. Lewis had a feel for how powerful his words could
become when he infused them with the drama and emotion of the
operas he loved. Though he lacked formal education, he was a vora-
cious reader of Shakespeare and classical literature, and developed a
knack for weaving their phrases into his speech.

As he grew into a young man, Lewis's body caught up with his voice. Everything about John L. Lewis was large: Throughout his life, fellow miners, newspaper reporters, and politicians found themselves intimidated by his sheer physical presence. His bushy eyebrows could make him seem terrifying to his opponents—or endearing to his allies.

On a trip west in 1903, Lewis witnessed one of the worst mining disasters of the era, when a spark in the Union Pacific Railroad coal mine in Hanna, Wyoming, caused a massive explosion and collapse. With other rescuers, Lewis helped pull survivors to safety—and to remove the bodies of the 169 men who had died in the accident. The mine owners blamed the miners themselves for the tragedy.

The horror of the mine explosion and the callous response of the mine owners had a deep impact on Lewis. When he returned home to Iowa, Lewis resolved to join the recently founded United Mine Workers of America. The union, he believed, was the only hope for miners.

American workers banded together to form the first unions in the nineteenth century. In those days, working people had to battle constantly against employers who paid them poor wages, treated them badly, and often forced them to work long hours. The first national labor union, the Knights of Labor, was founded secretly in 1869, by garment workers in Philadelphia who hoped to reduce their grueling working hours and increase their pay. The organization, which eventually reached out to workers in different industries and attracted a membership of over 750,000, proclaimed as its slogan "an injury to one is the concern of all." Alone, a worker was mostly powerless; in a union, workers stood some chance of making their voices heard.

John L. Lewis, circa 1921.
Harris & Ewing, photographer, Library of Congress, Prints and Photographs Division

Before the Crash, America's unions were on the run, harassed and bullied by business leaders, judges, and the police. The men who owned America's factories, mines, railroads, and meatpacking houses nearly always enjoyed the upper hand. And even though the government believed in leaving private business alone, it did step in now and then, sending soldiers or policemen when a factory owner or mine operator needed help keeping his workers in line.

But the unions never gave up. And in the early years of Roosevelt's presidency, it seemed as if their day had finally come. The spark that lit their fuse, in 1933, was a minor footnote to the National Industrial Recovery Act, titled Section 7a: *Employees shall have the right to organize and bargain collectively through representatives of their own choosing, and shall be free from the interference, restraint, or coercion of employers....*

For the first time in US history, the government was flashing a signal that it was officially on the side of working people—or at least neutral—in disputes with employers. Sensing the change of heart, working Americans everywhere made new and louder demands and joined unions in huge numbers. One government official sent an urgent telegram to Washington: THEY ARE UNION MAD, AND HAVE BEEN LED TO BELIEVE THAT THE GOVERNMENT UPHOLDS THEM IN THEIR STAND.

In fact, FDR had *not* come into office as a great supporter of unions. But in 1933 he sensed a change in the air and threw his weight behind them. FDR solidified his support for working people by signing the National Labor Relations Act of 1935 (known as the "Wagner

Striking cotton workers in California, in October 1933.
Powell Studio, Corcoran, California, Library of Congress, Prints and Photographs Division

Act," for Senator Robert Wagner of New York, who sponsored it in Congress). The Wagner Act guaranteed the right of workers to join a union, promoted "collective bargaining" between unions and employers, and established the National Labor Relations Board to referee disputes.

John L. Lewis—now president of the United Mine Workers—saw an opportunity. He believed that if the nation's millions of industrial workers could be invited to join one big union, all Americans would come together and battle the Depression by making sure that every worker was paid—and treated—fairly. In 1936, Lewis helped found the Congress of Industrial Organizations (CIO), which aimed to do just that.

John L. Lewis at a mine workers' meeting in Pennsylvania, striking the fighting pose that inspired respect and admiration.
Sheldon Dick, photographer, Library of Congress, Farm Security Administration/Office of War Information Collection, 1938

Not even Lewis had anticipated how enthusiastically workers would react to this idea. The CIO became an instant success: From autoworkers in Detroit to pecan shellers in San Antonio, workers clamored to join the new organization. Union membership became a patriotic duty and a way of signing on to the New Deal. America's millions of new union members viewed as their leader not just John L. Lewis but FDR himself.

Working people finally felt they were in a good position to claim a larger piece of the pie, more control over their lives, and more respect from their bosses. The only question that remained was: How could these things be won, when America's largest companies still refused

A poster promoting FDR's support for
labor unions, mid-1930s.
AFL-CIO Collections

to negotiate with unions? It would take a small group of brave men and women, working in the heart of America's biggest company, to lead the way forward.

Just before New Year's Eve 1936, a young woman working in the United Automobile Workers office in Flint, Michigan, flipped a switch. A bright red lightbulb flashed on.

The light was a secret signal, and soon workers streamed into the huge factory building next door, the General Motors Fisher Body Plant Number Two.

"She's ours!" a man shouted from a third-floor window. Bob Stinson, a worker in the plant, recalled that within five minutes, the whole factory had shut down. "The foreman was pretty well astonished," he remembered, adding that the workers "informed the supervisors they could stay, if they stayed in their office. They told the plant police they could do their job as long as they didn't interfere."

What the workers did next set off alarm bells all over the United States.

They sat down.

Sit-down strikers occupying the General Motors plant in Flint. "This strike has been coming for years," one of the strikers explained. "We are right, and when you're right you can't lose."
Sheldon Dick, photographer, Library of Congress, Farm Security Administration/Office of War Information Collection, 1937

All across the plant, men who just hours before had strained and sweated on automobile assembly lines, furiously piecing together General Motors' popular cars, now would not budge. The great Flint sit-down strike had begun.

General Motors, the largest company in the world, ground to a halt. It couldn't do what it wanted to do most—build and sell cars—if its own workers refused to cooperate.

The strike had been organized by the United Automobile Workers, a CIO union led by the brothers Walter and Victor Reuther. Lewis hurried to Detroit to lend his help. In the town of Flint itself, local people rallied to support the union.

The management of General Motors, though, was not going to give in so easily. Alfred Sloan, chairman of the company, tried to force Michigan governor Frank Murphy to send in National Guard troops. In the past, the government's intervention would have put a stop to the strike— but the New Deal had changed things.

John L. Lewis rushed straight to the governor's office and described—with the dramatic flair for which he was famous— what he would do if the government took sides:

Gather round me and I'll tell
* you all a story*
Of the Fisher Body Factory
. Number One
When the dies they started
* moving,*
The union men then had a
* meeting,*
To decide right then and there
* what must be done.*
The four thousand union boys,
They made a lot of noise,
They decided then and there to
* shut down tight.*
In the office they got snooty,
So we started picket duty,
Now the Fisher Body Shop is out
* on strike.*

—SONG RECORDED BY ALAN LOMAX

I shall personally enter General Motors; Chevrolet Plant Number Four. I shall order the men to disregard your order, to stand fast. I shall then walk up to the largest window in the plant, open it, divest myself of my outer raiment, remove my shirt, and bare my bosom. Then, when you order your troops to fire, mine will be the first breast those bullets will strike. And, as my body falls from the window to the ground, you will listen to the voice of your grandfather as he whispers in your ear, "Frank, are you sure you are doing the right thing?"

The governor hesitated and then held back.

Outraged, General Motors persuaded the local police force to move in; the strikers got word, and prepared their defenses. When policemen charged the Fisher Body Plant Number Two, firing tear gas and live ammunition, the strikers fought back, using improvised slingshots to hurl the heavy hinge joints used for attaching car doors.

People in Flint rally in front of the General Motors plant to support the sit-down strikers, 1937.
Walter P. Reuther Library, Archives of Labor and Urban Affairs, Wayne State University

The strikers dubbed it the "Battle of the Running Bulls." The next morning, Governor Murphy sent heavily armed National Guard troops to Flint to maintain order—but ordered them to leave the workers alone.

Michigan National Guardsmen confront strike supporters across the street from the General Motors plant in Flint, during the sit-down strike of 1937.
Walter P. Reuther Library, Archives of Labor and Urban Affairs, Wayne State University

The Flint strikers understood that something major had changed. That morning, singing echoed through the factories.

> C I O, C I O
> Here we go, we will grow, that we know,
> For our ranks are stronger,
> We're weak no longer
> We'll win our fight against the foe,
> CIO, CIO
> In the mills, in the shops, mines below,
> We know what's wise now, we'll organize now
> Into one big union
> The CIO.
>
> —A SONG RECORDED BY IDA AND WILLIAM RINAS
> DURING THE STRIKE

General Motors workers cheering at the end of the sit-down strike.
Walter P. Reuther Library, Archives of Labor and Urban Affairs, Wayne State University

On February 11, after a forty-four-day strike, John L. Lewis and General Motors signed an agreement respecting the right of the union to negotiate for the workers.

In the months that followed, the union won better wages, safer working conditions, and better treatment for the General Motors workers in Flint. And Lewis was just getting started. The CIO rode to victory in steel mills, meatpacking

CIO cotton mill workers on strike in Georgia.
Jack Delano, photographer, Library of Congress, Farm Security Administration/Office of War Information Collection, 1941

plants, and other factories across the United States. By 1939, more than eight million Americans belonged to unions—six million more than in 1929, when the Crash hit.

Pushed by ordinary working people, the New Deal was gradually making sure that more and more Americans shared the benefits of an improving economy. Urged on by the CIO and its millions of new members, FDR and Frances Perkins succeeded in making many of the union's demands the law of the land. In 1938, Congress passed the Fair Labor Standards Act (FLSA), which established a federal minimum wage, the forty-hour workweek, and overtime pay. It also outlawed child labor throughout the country.

A poster explaining the new prohibition of child labor in the United States, 1941.
National Archives, Records of the Children's Bureau

In the early years of the Depression, the future seemed to hold only suffering, insecurity, and poverty. Barely half a decade later, America's working men and women—many of them now union members—felt a new order taking shape. Steelworker John Sargent argued that the CIO victories transformed "not only the curse of the working man in this country, but also the nature of the relationship between the working man and the government and the working man and the boss, for all time." And textile worker Marianna Costa reflected on all that had changed since the difficult days of the early

Union members in the late 1930s putting up a billboard that contrasts unionized and non-unionized ("open shop") workplaces.
Walter P. Reuther Library, Archives of Labor and Urban Affairs, Wayne State University

1930s: "We accomplished union representation,...time-and-a-half, a five-day work week, work clothes, vacation pay—and of course later on was pension and group insurance—grievance procedure, no lay-offs unless you had arbitration.

"My God," Costa added, "it was a new world."

PART THREE
SETBACK

It was as though the sky was divided into two opposite worlds. On the south there was blue sky, golden sunlight and tranquility; on the north, there was a menacing curtain of boiling black dust that appeared to reach a thousand or more feet into the air.

—Pauline Winkler Grey, Meade County, Kansas

A dust storm rolls over Elkhart, Kansas, 1937.
Library of Congress, Farm Security Administration/Office of War Information Collection

Black Sunday dust storm in Kansas, 1935.
Kansas Historical Society

CHAPTER SEVEN
DARK CLOUDS

Just as the weight of the Depression began to lift over parts of America, more dark clouds appeared on the horizon.

For nearly five years, almost no rain had fallen in parts of Kansas, Oklahoma, and Texas. Drought crept across the huge expanse of dry grasslands, known as the Great Plains, which extended from Canada in the north all the way to Mexico in the south. By the mid-1930s, America's worst ecological disaster was in the making.

It could not have come at a worse time, heaping physical discomfort and suffering on top of a fragile economy.

On April 14, 1935, which came to be known as Black Sunday, a black dust cloud, so tall that it blocked out the sun and generated its own lightning and thunder, rolled south across Kansas, Oklahoma, and Texas. The National Weather Service reported that the storm turned "afternoon brightness immediately into midnight darkness, and absolutely zero visibility."

On Sunday in April, 1935, and I was grading papers; sitting at our kitchen window, the window faced the north. And I looked up and there was the blackest cloud you ever saw just about a third of the way from the horizon.

And by the time I got into the kitchen, halfway across the kitchen; to reach for the match-box, I couldn't see the matchbox. That dirt hit that quickly, and it just engulfed you, it just covered everything, and you couldn't see, you couldn't see anything.

—LOLA ADAMS CRUM, DODGE CITY, KANSAS

To some people that day, it seemed as if the end of the world had come.

A reporter named Robert Geiger had to drive with his car door open so that he could see enough to inch his way down the road. The next day, his report coined a new term: "Dust Bowl."

Without rain, the soil turned to dust, and powerful windstorms picked up that dust and carried it over the plains. Soon, dust blanketed thousands of square miles of the American heartland, smothering crops and burying livestock. "The dust drifted like snow," Winton Sipe of Kansas recalled. "It drifted about eighteen inches deep on the northeast side of all the buildings, and every fence post, tree and weed had a long, pointed drift on its northeast side."

Some of the storms lifted red dust high into the atmosphere and hurtled it east on wind currents. Red snow fell as far north as New England that winter.

Things were already bad for farmers, who were often deeply in debt to the banks that had lent them money for tractors and other

Black Sunday dust storm in Texas, 1935.
Franklin D. Roosevelt Presidential Library and Museum

machinery. Farming now became impossible on land that had been stripped of topsoil. For many people, the dust made already hard times completely unbearable.

From desperation or simple weariness, people started abandoning the Great Plains states. By the thousands, they loaded up Ford Model Ts and pickup trucks or boarded trains, most of them heading west to California. "Okies" and "Arkies"—farmers, laborers, doctors, teachers, and small businessmen alike—left in one of the largest mass migrations in American history. "My dad had a sale and we sold everything we owned," recalled Ethel Belezzuoli, who was born in

A father and his sons crossing their yard in Cimarron County, Oklahoma.
Arthur Rothstein, photographer, Library of Congress, Farm Security Administration/Office of War Information Collection, 1936

Marlow, Oklahoma, and migrated to California when she was sixteen. "We brought what we could on a little two-wheel trailer." Oscar Kludt's family traveled in "a big twelve-cylinder Nash, one car packed with ten people." All of their possessions were tied to the roof.

A newspaper deliveryman in Ness City, Kansas, wearing a gas mask to protect his eyes and lungs from the fine dust, in 1935.
Kansas Historical Society

A family from Oklahoma on the highway in California.
Dorothea Lange, photographer, Library of Congress, Farm Security Administration/Office of War Information Collection, 1937

The Dust Bowl migrants, almost three hundred thousand of them, followed Route 66 to California. "We didn't realize there were so many people on the road until we got out there," recalled Vera Criswell, who made the three-day trip with her family from Texas. Some people would camp along the side of the road along the way, while others would stay in sparsely furnished cabins rented by the night. On the long trip from Oklahoma, Loye Holmes's family "would camp at night and build little fires and do our cooking." The whole family slept on mattresses on the ground.

California's fertile San Joaquin Valley was bursting with an annual cotton crop that needed to be picked. Cotton growers welcomed cheap labor, but many others in California panicked at the huge influx of poor people. In 1936, Los Angeles's police chief sent one hundred fifty officers to the Arizona border, to create what he called a "bum blockade." "When they need us they call us migrants," one man complained, "and when we've picked their crop, we're bums and we got to get out."

Once in California, Okies found it difficult to settle in one place for long. They followed work, which meant going where the crops—lettuce, peas, grapes, cotton, pears, peaches, plums, celery—needed picking. On the move, and working for as little as $3 per twelve-hour day, the Dust Bowl migrants scraped by like refugees in a foreign country. They set up temporary camps, completely out in the open and exposed to the weather. Many parked near polluted irrigation ditches. With no access to clean water or sanitation, people fell ill with typhoid, malaria, tuberculosis, and other life-threatening diseases. An investigator for the federal government found "filth, squalor, and entire absence of sanitation, and a crowding of human beings into totally inadequate tents or crude structures built of boards, weeds, and anything that was found at hand...."

The rear view of a migrant family's truck, parked by the side of the road near Bakersfield, California.

Dorothea Lange, photographer, Library of Congress, Farm Security Administration/Office of War Information Collection, 1939

"We would find either side of the highway just dotted with these old, beat-up cars, some of them had just barely gasped over the mountain," a doctor from Kern County Hospital in Bakersfield, California, recalled. She described the Okie migrants she treated as "wind swept people," with "a leathery toughness about their skin." Their bodies were marked by lives of hard work and deprivation. "The women looked twenty years older than they really were," she remarked.

From February to March of 1936, the photographer Dorothea

> *I'D RATHER NOT BE ON RELIEF*
> *We go around all dressed in rags*
> *While the rest of the world goes*
> *   neat,*
> *And we have to be satisfied*
> *With half enough to eat.*
> *We have to live in lean-tos,*
> *Or else we live in a tent,*
> *For when we buy our bread and*
> *   beans*
> *There's nothing left for rent.*
>
> —SONG TRANSCRIBED IN A MIGRANT
>   WORKER CAMP IN CALIFORNIA

Two girls from a family of Oklahoma Dust Bowl refugees, stranded on a highway in California in June 1935. According to the photographer, Dorothea Lange, they were part of a "family of six; [with] no shelter, no food, no money and almost no gasoline."
Dorothea Lange, photographer, Library of Congress, Farm Security Administration/Office of War Information Collection

Lange spent a month taking photographs of the migrant laborers in California. Lange was working for the Resettlement Administration, a New Deal agency that built camps for the impoverished Dust Bowl refugees. Near Nipomo, California, Lange came across Florence Owens Thompson and her children living in a makeshift tent. "She told me her age, that she was thirty-two," Lange recalled. "She said that they had been living on frozen vegetables from the surrounding fields, and birds that the children killed. She had just sold the tires from her car to buy food."

Migrant Mother appeared in magazines, books, and eventually on a US postage stamp. Although Lange's photograph made Florence

Florence Owens Thompson and her family.
Dorothea Lange, photographer, Library of Congress, Farm Security Administration/Office of War Information Collection, 1936

Owens Thompson the most recognizable symbol of the white Okie migration to California, in reality, Thompson was Native American, born a Cherokee on a reservation in Oklahoma. At the time the photograph was taken, she had ten children; her husband and several of

This photograph of Florence Owens Thompson and her children, titled *Migrant Mother*, became the most famous image of the Great Depression.
Dorothea Lange, photographer, Library of Congress, Farm Security Administration/Office of War Information Collection, 1936

the children were away, getting their car fixed. Thompson and her large family picked crops all over the state, migrating to wherever they could find work. In the camp where Lange snapped her photo, close to 2,500 migrant workers neared starvation, after a sudden freeze had killed the pea crop. "The look of hunger was already in the camp," according to Thompson's grandson, who remembered his grandmother's stories about that time, and "within a week death would be there too. First, the very young, and the very old. Soon the locals would descend on the camp, arresting some, beating others, but scattering all to the four winds." (A news reporter discovered Thompson many years later, in 1978, living in a trailer park in California. The subject of the most famous image of the Great Depression survived entirely on her monthly Social Security check of $331.60.)

Another artist investigating the plight of the Dust Bowl migrants was a writer and journalist named John Steinbeck. In October 1936, the *San Francisco News* hired Steinbeck to write a series of articles that told the story of the Resettlement Administration camps. Steinbeck wrote with great sympathy about the lives the migrants led, and about the choices forced on them by economic conditions beyond their control. In the Weedpatch Camp in Arvin, California, Steinbeck became riveted by the tragedy of one particular family, which he described with an authentic detail that was similar to Dorothea Lange's photography:

> When the ranch dried up and blew away the family
> put its moveable possession in an old Dodge truck and
> came to California. They arrived in time for the orange

picking in Southern California and put in a good average season.

The older boy and the father together made $60. At that time the automobile broke out some teeth of the differential and the repairs, together with three second-hand tires, took $22. The family moved into Kern County to chop grapes and camped in the squatters' camp on the edge of Bakersfield.

At this time the father sprained his ankle and the little girl developed measles. Doctors' bills amounted to $10 of the remaining store, and food and transportation took most of the rest....

The father now applied for relief and found that he was ineligible because he had not established the necessary residence. All resources were gone. A little food was given to the family by neighbors in the squatters' camp....

Steinbeck's reporting in the Weedpatch Camp inspired his epic novel *The Grapes of Wrath*, the tale of the fictional Joad family's descent into poverty after migrating to California. *The Grapes of Wrath* became the best-selling book of 1939, and the most influential book of the entire decade. The Joads' plight dramatized the wounds the Great Depression had inflicted, not just on individual people but on the very idea of American independence.

Steinbeck, Lange, and other witnesses to the Dust Bowl tragedy

In this photograph, Tom Collins, the manager of the Kern migrant camp, speaks with a mother and baby from a family who had fled the Dust Bowl. Collins assisted the novelist John Steinbeck with his reporting in California, and the camp that appears in *The Grapes of Wrath* is modeled after the camp in this image.
Dorothea Lange, photographer, Library of Congress, Farm Security Administration/Office of War Information Collection, 1936

shocked Americans' consciences. They even triggered a congressional investigation into the conditions in California's fields. But despite this exposure, the migrants kept coming—and kept finding themselves treated as outsiders, excluded from the New Deal and its message of hope for a better America.

CHAPTER EIGHT
THE BLIND SPOT

On October 22, 1934—as the New Deal was getting into high gear and Frances Perkins penned her first draft of the Social Security plan—an African American man from Marianna, Florida, named Claude Neal was arrested for the murder of Lola Cannady, a white woman. Neal and Cannady were neighbors, and had known each other since they were children. They may have been in a romantic relationship, but that evidence, like all evidence in this case, never made it to a courtroom—because Claude Neal was never brought to trial.

The sheriff who had arrested Neal, Flake Chambliss, spirited him out of Marianna when rumors began to spread that a mob was gathering to kill the imprisoned suspect. Neal was eventually locked up in an Alabama jail nearly two hundred miles away—but even that wasn't enough to save him. Under suspicious circumstances, a group of armed men broke into the jail and hauled Neal all the way back to Marianna.

The fate that awaited Claude Neal was no secret. Local newspapers carried the story of his "capture." A nearby radio station invited "all white people" to come and watch Neal die. Soon, telegrams spread

word all over the United States; a *New York Times* headline warned,
"Mob Holds Negro; Invitations Issued For Lynch Party." The governor
of Florida was alerted but decided not to get involved.

On Friday night, October 26, in front of several thousand spectators (including many children), Claude Neal was gruesomely
murdered in a public lynching. Soon afterward, a white mob turned
on the black community of Marianna, attacking and injuring dozens,
burning homes, and wrecking businesses. The governor of Florida
sent in the National Guard to put down the rioting, but much too late
to save Claude Neal.

Nobody was charged in the killing of Claude Neal; a local grand
jury determined that he died "at the hands of persons unknown to us."

The lynching of Claude Neal and the violence that followed outraged many Americans, including President Roosevelt himself. Yet
these were not uncommon events in the South during the 1930s.

During the Great Depression, most of America's black citizens could not vote, travel freely, or live where they wished. They
had almost no hope of achieving the American dream. All over the
South—where most African Americans still lived during the 1930s—
black people were subjected to a harsh system of racial segregation
laws, sometimes called "Jim Crow." Jim Crow laws determined where
black people could buy their groceries, whom they could marry, and
even whom they could speak to.

After the Crash, white southerners tried to push black people down
even further. Black people were the first to be fired and the last to receive

A sharecropper in Montgomery County, Alabama, with a horse-drawn plow.
Arthur Rothstein, photographer, Library of Congress, Farm Security Administration/Office of War Information Collection, 1937

desperately needed relief. In cities across the United States, more than *twice* as many African Americans lost their jobs during the Depression as white people. And those who clung to regular work found that more effort was expected from them, usually for less pay. Lillie Fenner, a farm worker in Halifax County, North Carolina, remembered that her landlord "just wanted you to stay in the field working all the time…they didn't want you to go and get a cool drink of water."

A segregated movie theater in Belzoni, Mississippi, showing a separate entrance for "colored" viewers.

Marion Post Walcott, photographer, Library of Congress, Farm Security Administration/Office of War Information Collection, late 1930s

Jim Crow forced black people into a separate and unequal existence, forbidding them from taking part in the new America FDR was trying to build. And lynching was the white South's answer to anyone who dared resist.

In the opening years of the Great Depression, the number of lynchings spiked sharply, especially in the South. There were ten reported lynchings in 1929, twenty-one in 1930, and twenty-eight in 1933.

One of the bravest people to challenge lynching during the Great Depression was a man named Walter White. On the eve of the Crash, in 1929, White became president of the National Association for the Advancement of Colored People, or NAACP, an organization founded in 1909 to defend the rights of African Americans against racist oppression and violence.

Walter White often reflected on how a quirk of his appearance so dramatically shaped the course of his life. The son of two black parents (both of whom had been born into slavery), Walter nevertheless appeared white to almost everyone he met. His light skin, straight

Walter White, who joined the NAACP in 1918 and eventually became its president. White helped lead the civil rights struggles of the 1930s, bringing the issue of racial equality to the nation's attention.
Gordon Parks, photographer, Library of Congress, Farm Security Administration/Office of War Information Collection, 1942

blond hair, and blue eyes permitted him at times to escape the harshest effects of the racial color line in his hometown of Atlanta, Georgia. Yet, having witnessed the daily slights and indignities to his family and friends, Walter always understood that he was undeniably African American. At a young age, he committed himself to fighting for equal treatment for black people, at a time in history when this seemed an almost impossible dream.

White joined the staff of the NAACP in 1918, at a time when lynchings had reached epidemic proportions across the South. In response, NAACP president James Weldon Johnson came up with the idea of sending White on undercover missions to investigate lynching crime scenes, posing as a white newspaper reporter. Walter's ambiguous appearance proved a unique asset, enabling him to move freely through both black and white neighborhoods as he sought to uncover the truth of what happened in segregated southern towns.

White turned out to be an exceptionally clever spy. His particular skill was to trick unsuspecting killers into bragging openly about their crimes; he was so persuasive that one lynch mob actually deputized him and told him to kill black people on sight (he escaped before the mob discovered his true identity). Another time, White pretended to be a newspaper reporter for the *New-York Evening Post*, in order to get an audience with the governor of Georgia, to inform him in person about a particularly vicious lynching. Across the 1920s, White traveled thousands of miles on behalf of the NAACP, investigating forty-one lynchings and eight race riots.

After each undercover investigation, White would publish dramatic newspaper accounts of the lynching, systematically exposing the perpetrators as well as the local officials who allowed these murders to happen. White's stirring newspaper articles helped make him a hero to black communities across the country.

Over time, White used his newfound status to do something the NAACP needed most, which was to sign up new members and establish new NAACP branches—in Nashville, New Orleans, and dozens of other cities and towns. In 1929, White's singular combination of courage, persuasiveness, and organizational skills pushed him into

Flag hanging from the NAACP offices in New York City, in 1936.
Library of Congress, Prints and Photographs Division

the spotlight as one of the nation's most important and effective civil rights leaders.

By the time Claude Neal was murdered in Florida, Walter White had worked for more than a decade and a half to force America to pay attention to the crime of lynching. But during the long years of the Great Depression, one case above all helped keep the crime of lynching in the public eye, and would eventually spark a widespread effort to end it once and for all.

Though it played out across the entire decade of the 1930s, the "Scottsboro Boys" case began in the earliest days of the Great Depression, in a small town in Alabama.

The Scottsboro case originated with a fight that broke out between a group of young black and white men on a freight train approaching Paint Rock, Alabama, on its way from Chattanooga to Memphis, Tennessee. Like so many trains crisscrossing the country in 1931, this one was packed with hoboes—men, boys, and in this case women traveling far from home, hoping to find a day's work or a free meal. Thirteen-year-old Roy Wright was riding the train that night with his older brother, Andy, in the hopes of finding work. It was the first time Roy had left his home in Chattanooga.

One of the black men riding the train, Haywood Patterson, claimed that a group of white men had threatened to eject the African American hoboes, saying that "this was a white man's train." After some shoving, two white men fell from the train and reported to a local sheriff that they had been attacked. Later that night, a posse of armed white men met the train at the Paint Rock station and arrested nine young black men, including Roy and Andy Wright.

From that moment on, Wright and eight other young men entered a world of fear and terror. They soon learned that the worst possible accusation had been leveled against them: In the confused hours following their arrest, two white women—also riding the train that night—had falsely accused the group of rape.

Outside the jail, a mob of hundreds of white men threatened to lynch Roy, his brother, and their seven unlucky companions. "I knew if a white woman accused a black man of rape," one of the companions recalled, "he was as good as dead."

The group was put into metal shackles and tossed onto a flatbed truck, which drove off before the crowd could get to them. As readers of Walter White's reporting knew well, the nine "Scottsboro Boys"—named for the Alabama town where their trial took place—had stumbled into one of Jim Crow's most dangerous traps. Having narrowly escaped being killed at the hands of a lynch mob, southern "justice" caught up with them barely two weeks later. Their hasty trials included false testimony from witnesses; hostile, all-white juries; and a biased judge. All were found guilty, and all but twelve-year-old Roy were sentenced to death by the electric chair. The judge sentenced Roy to life behind bars.

In this instance, however, the Scottsboro Boys discovered that they were not alone. Word had gotten out about their arrests, and the news traveled as far as New York City. They quickly became a national sensation, with African American church leaders, artists, politicians, and activists around the country rallying to their defense.

In the depths of the Depression, with so little to lose and so much at stake, black people everywhere resolved to fight back.

A group called the International Labor Defense (ILD), supported by the Communist Party, hastily arranged for an appeal of the Scottsboro convictions. After months of maneuvering, the case went all

Eight of the nine Scottsboro Boys pictured in prison in 1936, along with NAACP representatives Juanita Jackson Mitchell, Laura Kellum, and Dr. Ernest W. Taggart.
Smithsonian Institution, National Portrait Gallery

the way to the US Supreme Court, which ruled that the nine men had not received a fair trial.

Eleanor Roosevelt followed the case closely. Charles Hamilton Houston, perhaps the most respected civil rights lawyer of his time, wrote that the case affected "every Negro in the country...and demands our complete and undivided support until the last Scottsboro boy is free." And Walter White was determined to use the Scottsboro case to bring the issue of lynching to the attention of politicians in the nation's capital.

Save the Scottsboro Boys

Death Stalks at Scottsboro
Come to the Scottsboro
MASS MEETING
—at—
Vermont Ave. Baptist Church
(Vermont Ave. bet. Q and R Sts., N.W.)
Monday, February 10, at 8 P. M.
HEAR
Congressman Vito Marcantonio, of New York.
Thurman L. Dodson, President of the D.C. Bar Association.
Prof. Ralph Bunche, of Howard University.
Nannie L. Burroughs.
Ex-Senator Smith W. Brookhart.
Rev. W. H. Thomas, Pastor of Metropolitan A.M.E. Church.
Rev. C. T. Murray, Pastor of Vermont Ave. Baptist Church.

Sponsored by the local provisional Scottsboro Committee.
Mrs. Virginia McGuire, Chairman
Mrs. Isadora Letcher, Treasurer

Admission   -   -   Free

A flyer advertising one of the many hundreds of meetings organized in support of the Scottsboro Boys.
UCLA Library Special Collections

After years of new trials and, in some cases, long prison sentences, all nine Scottsboro Boys were eventually freed from Alabama jails. Roy Wright grew into manhood in jail, spending six years in total behind bars, including one thirteen-month stretch in solitary confinement—all for a crime he did not commit. Before his release at age nineteen he told a visitor that "if I have to spend more than one or two years longer, I just as well spend the rest of my life. If I was an old man perhaps I wouldn't mind it so much but that's what's against

> *A young girl named Harper Lee lived just a few hours south of Scottsboro in the 1930s; her blockbuster book,* To Kill a Mockingbird, *may well be modeled after the events surrounding the trial.*

me; I'm young and innocent of the crime."

The Scottsboro case was the most-watched legal battle of the Great Depression. Many observers, including journalists, poets, musicians, novelists, and politicians, drew lessons from it about new possibilities for stopping the violence against black people. The Scottsboro trials had triggered something that was about much more than nine innocent men: For the first time since the rise of Jim Crow in the 1890s, a national debate broke out over whether the nation should treat African Americans equally.

African Americans everywhere joined in the struggle against Jim Crow. Most of the South's black people used the same weapons they had wielded for almost thirty years: their feet. What some call the "Great Migration" had been under way long before the 1930s. But as the Depression made living conditions in the South even more oppressive for black people, many more of them decided to leave. The flow of people grew, until by the end of the 1930s, cities like Chicago had become a promised land, overflowing with hundreds of thousands of black migrants. They followed the train lines, riding the Illinois Central Railroad and other routes out of the South.

News from the North made its way into the smallest southern towns, often by word of mouth via black railroad workers or by African American newspapers such as the *Chicago Defender*, that black people were building new lives away from Jim Crow. In the relative freedom of the North, they built churches, grocery stores, dance halls, restaurants, insurance companies, newspapers, funeral homes, and more.

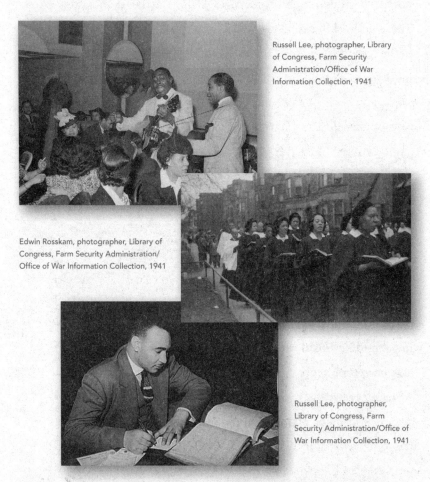

Russell Lee, photographer, Library of Congress, Farm Security Administration/Office of War Information Collection, 1941

Edwin Rosskam, photographer, Library of Congress, Farm Security Administration/Office of War Information Collection, 1941

Russell Lee, photographer, Library of Congress, Farm Security Administration/Office of War Information Collection, 1941

One group of New Deal photographers, working with the famous novelist Richard Wright, spent months telling the story of the African American neighborhood in Chicago nicknamed "Bronzeville."

For the first time, these black migrants did something Jim Crow had forbidden them to do in the South: They registered to vote. In the 1936 presidential race—the first since the New Deal was launched, and a national test of its popularity—African American voters in northern cities became crucial to FDR and the Democratic Party. These poorest, least powerful Americans suddenly had the attention of the nation's leaders in Washington, DC, and they voted overwhelmingly for FDR, helping him achieve his second landslide victory.

Nevertheless, the nation's capital, itself a segregated, southern city, was slow to change. Despite its many accomplishments, the New Deal had a major blind spot. Due to the power of southern white senators and congressmen in Washington, the most important New Deal programs almost completely ignored African Americans.

And yet black people also had one key ally in Washington who just happened to live inside the White House.

Years before, Eleanor

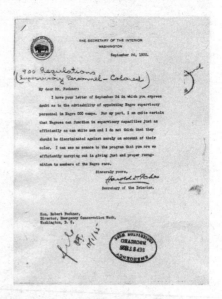

The CCC, which had saved hundreds of thousands of young people from desperate circumstances, openly discriminated against black people. This 1935 letter from Secretary of the Interior Harold Ickes pushed for the inclusion of African American supervisors in the CCC.
National Archives and Records Administration

Roosevelt had met Mary McLeod Bethune, the pioneering civil rights activist, educator, and founder of Bethune-Cookman University in Daytona Beach, Florida. The two met regularly, traveled together, and became close friends. Bethune taught her friend about the painful realities of racial discrimination in the United States, and as a result Eleanor Roosevelt became a brave and lifelong advocate for equality. In 1934, Eleanor announced that, for the first time in American history, the White House would be integrated.

Roosevelt pushed for Bethune's appointment as director of the Division of Negro Affairs of the National Youth Administration, a position that put Bethune in charge of creating jobs and offering support to young black people under the New Deal.

Working together with Bethune, Eleanor Roosevelt also gathered together what came to be known as the "Black Cabinet," an informal but influential group of African American advisers and political leaders who sought to guide the president on issues important to African Americans.

At a time when they were legally excluded from

Mary McLeod Bethune during her time at the National Youth Administration.
Gordon Parks, photographer, Library of Congress, Farm Security Administration/Office of War Information Collection, 1943

restaurants, bus stations, schools, and hotels in Washington (and almost everywhere else), African Americans now had an open door at the White House. FDR was no champion of racial equality or civil rights, but Eleanor kept the pressure on her husband.

Working together with Walter White and the NAACP, Eleanor lobbied Franklin hard to support the Costigan-Wagner Bill (named for its sponsors, Senators Edward Costigan of Colorado and Robert F. Wagner of New York), which would make lynching a federal crime and bring the power of the federal government into the states to help prevent it. In early January 1935, White wrote to Eleanor that "to all of those who have spoken to me about it, I have urged patience, saying that perhaps the President will send a specific message to Congress on lynching or include specific recommendation for the passage of

President Franklin D. Roosevelt's "Black Cabinet" in 1938.
Scurlock Studio, photographer, Smithsonian Institution, National Museum of American History

the Costigan-Wagner bill." But FDR crushed their hopes, arguing privately that the bill would offend white southern politicians and endanger support for his New Deal policies.

In almost unimaginably harsh and dangerous circumstances, African Americans found ways to stand up for their rights, doing everything they could to keep the question of racial equality on the front pages of the nation's newspapers. Walter White devoted the NAACP's talent and resources to attacking segregation head-on. Throughout the remaining years of the Depression, NAACP lawyers could be found in courtrooms across the South, defending black people unjustly accused of crimes; filing lawsuits challenging segregation in schools; and working on cases to support the right of black people to vote in elections. They braved hostile juries and threats by local sheriffs and often traveled secretly over long distances to do their work. One of these lawyers was a young Thurgood Marshall, who eventually argued the Supreme Court case *Brown v. Board of Education of Topeka*, which outlawed segregation in 1954. He would go on to become a Supreme Court justice.

Though it did not yet have a name, a movement had begun during the Great Depression to end Jim Crow in the United States. For the remainder of the 1930s, African Americans and their white allies struggled—against overwhelming odds, and usually without success—to end lynching, roll back racial segregation, and achieve equal treatment.

CHAPTER NINE
ENEMIES

The Great Depression turned out to be a stubborn foe. In some parts of the country, harsh conditions settled into a grueling, daily reality, despite the efforts of FDR and the New Deal to improve people's lives. Throughout these long, stormy years, many Americans came to believe that *someone* was to blame for the nation's troubles. A new group of vocal critics turned to the radio to broadcast their ideas. For much of the 1930s, the airwaves crackled with accusations, conspiracies, and voices of protest.

The hunt for enemies was on.

Early in the Depression, most Americans had blamed Wall Street fat cats for the Crash and the Depression that followed. One citizen from Pottstown, Pennsylvania, wrote a letter to the White House that echoed the concerns of millions, asserting, "I hope that Wall St will never have the power again to cause such a panic...I hope the guilty gang will be punished before they die. I say this whole panic was brought on by dishonest group which I hope will be punished...."

A Mexican mother and her child in California. "Sometimes I tell my children that I would like to go [back] to Mexico, but they tell me, 'We don't want to go, we belong here.'"
Dorothea Lange, photographer, Library of Congress, Farm Security Administration/Office of War Information Collection, 1935

As time passed, however, some looked around and found the causes of their troubles living right next door.

Even though America was a country of immigrants, native-born Americans—who were sometimes the children of immigrants themselves—often blamed newcomers for the nation's problems. These feelings had come to a head in 1924, when Congress passed the Johnson-Reed Act, which cut off nearly all immigration to the United States. As the number of jobs dwindled in the 1930s, feelings of resentment only grew. And suspicions now targeted one of the nation's largest groups of recent immigrants, from America's southern neighbor.

Mexican immigrants lived all across America in the 1930s, but especially in the states of the Southwest, and California in particular (which less than ninety years earlier had been part of Mexico itself). They toiled as fruit pickers in California, in meatpacking factories in Chicago, and on cattle ranches and sugar beet farms in Colorado, most often in appalling conditions, and at the lowest pay. Some were citizens of the United States, while others migrated seasonally—and all had family members in both countries.

As the Depression set in, local authorities all over the country, and particularly in California, Arizona, and Texas, began staging deportation raids against Mexican people. Some were arrested on city streets and herded onto trains bound for Mexico; others were

A Mexican miner and his child in Scotts Run, West Virginia.
Marion Post Wolcott, photographer, Library of Congress, Farm Security Administration/Office of War Information
Collection, 1938

simply intimidated into leaving. When she took over as secretary of labor, Frances Perkins found that the Labor Department staff were "operating all over this country shaking down immigrants, scaring them to death, making raids on their stores, their dance halls, their private dwellings."

On February 26, 1931, immigration agents surrounded a popular park in Los Angeles called La Placita, interrogating more than four hundred people of Mexican descent and arresting many of them. It wasn't an isolated incident; similar raids targeted Mexican people at home, in restaurants, and in their workplaces. In San Fernando, California, one woman remembered a raid on Ash

Wednesday as "the day of judgment," when "the *marciales*, deputy sheriffs, arrived in the late afternoon when the men were returning home from working in the lemon groves." The deputies arrested men at random, and barricaded the roads leading into the neighborhood, so that nobody could escape.

Another tactic for pressuring Mexicans to leave the United States became known as "repatriation," by which local organizations in Los Angeles, Detroit, and elsewhere "invited" people to leave voluntarily—even offering them one-way train tickets to Mexico. It was not a friendly invitation, however, for the threat of violence always hung over the repatriation campaigns. The journalist Cary McWilliams was at the train station in Los Angeles, California, where the first repatriations took place, and described a tearful scene of families that arrived "by the truckload—men, women, and children—with dogs, cats, and goats...half-open suitcases, rolls of bedding, and lunch baskets." Los Angeles County eventually sponsored fifteen trains, which carried nearly thirteen thousand people over the border to Mexico. Overall, four hundred thousand people of Mexican descent were expelled from the United States in the 1930s. Some people estimate that more than *half* of these were American citizens.

Mexicans were not the only targets of repatriation attempts. The Filipino Repatriation Act of 1935 offered money to any Filipino man who would voluntarily return to the Philippines. Few Filipinos accepted the offer, quietly resisting by simply staying put. But the message had been sent: Immigrants were not welcome.

Of all the voices sounding the warning about enemies in America, none was louder than that of Father Charles Coughlin, a Catholic priest and pastor of the National Shrine of the Little Flower in Royal Oak, Michigan. From a radio studio inside his small church, Coughlin built a huge national audience of radio listeners, through weekly broadcasts that eventually reached thirty million people; he may have had the largest radio audience in the world. In 1934, Coughlin received over ten thousand letters per day from his listeners, many of them stuffed with small financial contributions for his church (he was reported to have once made a deposit at his local bank of $20,000—in one-dollar bills).

At first, Coughlin was one of FDR's biggest cheerleaders, coining one of the memorable phrases of the era: "It is either Roosevelt or ruin!" He preached that American capitalism had

My family lived in Erie [Colorado] and my father had taken me along to shop in Longmont. I think I was about seven or eight or so; it was about 1935 or 1936. I witnessed police escorting Mexican families out of Longmont in a caravan. The police would stop occasionally and grab any Mexican-looking individual and throw them onto one of the trucks if they lacked identification. I realized the police weren't distinguishing between citizen and non-citizen. If you were Mexican, you were gone.

—EMMA GOMEZ MARTINEZ, LONGMONT, COLORADO

Father Coughlin delivers one of his radio broadcasts at the height of his popularity.
An Historical Exploration of Father Charles E. Coughlin's Influence, University of Detroit Mercy Special Collections

run amok, destroying the lives of ordinary Americans, while enriching the bankers who had gambled on Wall Street. Roosevelt's New Deal, Coughlin believed, was America's only salvation.

In the early years of FDR's presidency, Father Coughlin lent crucial support to New Deal programs. His endorsement carried weight: A radio station in New York City in 1934 asked listeners to name "the most useful citizen of the United Stated politically," other than FDR. Fifty-five percent voted for Coughlin.

Coughlin's enthusiasm for FDR cooled over time, however. The cause may well have been personal, for Coughlin resented the fact that the president did not offer him a role in the government, and perceived that Roosevelt was keeping him at arm's length. "He said he would rely on me," Coughlin complained, and that he "would be an important advisor. But he was a liar."

Coughlin turned against Roosevelt, at a time when he also revealed a paranoid and dangerous side to his political views. In his weekly radio broadcasts, he asserted that the New Deal was a Communist

A couple in Michigan listen to Father Coughlin's broadcast while reading his
weekly newsletter *Social Justice*, which peddled conspiracy theories as the
Depression dragged on.
Arthur S. Siegel, photographer, Library of Congress, Farm Security Administration/Office of War Information
Collection, 1939

conspiracy controlled by Jews. Coughlin even used his weekly newspaper to serialize the notorious anti-Semitic pamphlet "The Protocols
of the Elders of Zion," a fictitious document peddled by the billionaire
auto manufacturer Henry Ford, which depicted a conspiracy of Jewish bankers bent on dominating the world. Declaring that "someone
must be blamed" for the nation's lingering economic woes, Coughlin
helped poison the well of public opinion and encouraged the search
for enemies inside the United States.

In the late 1930s, as many people nervously followed the rise of the Nazi Party in Germany, Coughlin devoted more and more of his energy to promoting anti-Semitism and to opposing US involvement in international affairs. Through such efforts, Coughlin and his allies helped delay America's confrontation with the fascism menacing Europe, and the world. In 1938, he helped spur the creation of the Christian Front, a military-style organization that promised to protect America from Communists and Jews; a year later, the Christian Front held a huge anti-Semitic rally at Madison Square Garden in New York City.

A car parked on a street in Omaha, Nebraska, in 1938. The sign in the windshield advertises the owner's membership in the Bund, a pro-Nazi German American organization that attracted nearly ten thousand members during the Great Depression.
John Vachon, photographer, Library of Congress, Farm Security Administration/Office of War Information Collection

Finally, when war broke out in Europe in 1939, many people started questioning Father Coughlin's message and (in some cases) even his loyalties as an American. The Catholic Church forced him to cancel his broadcasts. He quickly faded from the scene, a resentful and angry figure who never forgave Franklin Roosevelt.

Coughlin's massive popularity, however, revealed a basic truth about America. Anti-Semitism had found a home in the United States—a fact that would have tragic consequences as Hitler's persecution of European Jews picked up speed.

On the night of November 9–10, 1938, Nazi gangs, encouraged by Adolf Hitler, went on a violent rampage against Jewish homes, businesses, and synagogues all over Germany, Austria, and the Sudetenland (a region of Czechoslovakia that had been annexed by Germany only two months earlier). Because of the glass shards that blanketed the streets the next morning, the night became known around the world as *Kristallnacht*, or "night of the broken glass." The traumatic events of that night convinced many German Jews that it was time to leave their homeland. Thousands of German Jews scrambled to emigrate, with many setting their sights on the United States.

The steamship MS *St. Louis* arrived in Havana, Cuba, on May 27 of that year, loaded with more than nine hundred German Jewish families and their belongings.

When the Cuban authorities refused to let the refugees off the ship, the *St. Louis* headed north to Miami. In Washington, American Jewish leaders frantically tried to get the US authorities to admit

The news of the past few days from Germany
has shocked public opinion in the United States.
Such news from any part of the world would in-
evitably produce a similar reaction among the
American people. With a view to gaining a firsthand picture of the situation in Germany I asked
the Secretary of State to order our Ambassador
in Berlin for report and consultation.

I myself could scarcely believe
that such things could occur in
a Twentieth Century civilization.

A statement made by FDR to the press on November 15, 1938, expressing
anger over the anti-Semitic attacks in Germany; his handwritten notes read "I
myself could scarcely believe that such things could occur in a twentieth century
civilization."

the refugees, but the State Department would not make an exception to its strict immigration rules. The US Coast Guard even sent two ships to guard the *St. Louis* off the coast of Florida, with orders to prevent any person from reaching the shore.

The *New York Times* called the MS *St. Louis* "the saddest ship afloat." Passengers could see the lights of Miami, but as the days passed, they were gripped with fear as the prospect of returning to Europe seemed increasingly likely.

You know, we always cling to the hope something is going to happen. They're not going to let us rot on the ocean. I mean, something had to happen to us. Of course, the fear was that we would go back to Germany. That was the big thing you know....

We just saw the Coast Guard boats surround us near Miami to make sure that we wouldn't even come close to the border, to the...to shore, so that was out. So we saw the lights of Miami. We saw the lights of America and that was it. So we slowly sailed back to Europe.

—GERDA BLACHMANN WILCHFORT

The *St. Louis* eventually ran out of options. Its captain managed to release passengers in ports all over western Europe. Some survived the war—but probably half perished in the Holocaust.

The *St. Louis* passengers were only a few of those people who fell victim to America's hunt for enemies. Even as FDR and his New Deal struggled to unite people against the Great Depression, the suspicion and fear of immigrants—and others—threatened to pull the nation in a different direction and to divide its citizens from one another.

The MS *St. Louis* in Havana Harbor.
National Archives and Records Administration

As the 1930s drew to a close, war and persecution engulfed the world beyond America's coasts.

On nearly every continent, totalitarian governments were gaining power and setting their sights on dominating the globe. The Empire of Japan invaded China in 1937, the first stop in what would become a massive conquest of nearly all of Asia, from Korea in the north to Papua New Guinea in the South Pacific. Italy, led by the fascist dictator Benito Mussolini, conquered Ethiopia in 1936. Nazi Germany annexed Austria in 1938, then quickly followed with the annexation of Czechoslovakia and military invasion of Poland in 1939—and these were just the beginning. Soon, all of Europe and Asia would be under attack by the "Axis" powers of Japan, Germany, and Italy.

Insulated by two oceans and thousands of sea miles to the nearest conflict zone, many Americans wished to steer a neutral course. The lingering Depression left some with no appetite for stepping into the conflict overseas. And others continued the campaign to snuff out perceived threats within US borders. But the Axis powers gathered more and more strength just over the horizon. And in ways no one could predict in 1939 and 1940, America's hidden path out of the Great Depression led straight into the fires of the coming world war.

PART FOUR

VICTORY

This nation has placed its destiny in the
hands and heads and hearts of its millions
of free men and women; and its faith
in freedom under the guidance of God.
Freedom means the supremacy of human
rights everywhere. Our support goes to
those who struggle to gain those rights
or keep them. *Our strength is our unity of
purpose* [emphasis added].

—FDR's STATE OF THE UNION ADDRESS,
JANUARY 6, 1941

Irma Lee McElroy paints an American insignia on the wing of an airplane, at Naval
Air Station Corpus Christi, in Texas, in 1942.
Howard R. Hollem, photographer, Library of Congress, Office of War Information Collection

PSNY 3-7-41 25M

Original

U. NAVAL AIR STATION, KODIAK ALASKA
NAVAL COMMUNICATIONS

Heading   NPC NR 63 F L Z F5L 071830 C8Q TART 0 BT

From:	CINCPAC	Date	7 DEC 41

To: ALL SHIPS PRESENT AT HAWAIIN AREA.

Info: - U R G E N T -

DEFERRED unless otherwise checked	ROUTINE	PRIORITY	AIRMAIL	MAILGRAM

AIRRAID ON REARLHARBOR X THIS IS NO DRILL

07014

RM 58 1910 7DEC

Comdg Off	Exec	Comm	Oper	Supply	Disb	Med'l	Aerog	Pers	Pub Wks	Mar Det	A & R	Files	FAD	NRAB	OOD	WDO

A–Denotes action   I–Denotes information   X–Denotes copy only

The transcript of a radio message first reporting the Pearl Harbor attack, on December 7, 1941.
National Archives and Records Administration

CHAPTER TEN

A WAR TO DEFEAT THE DEPRESSION

On December 7, 1941, the Imperial Japanese Navy launched a surprise attack on the US naval base at Pearl Harbor, Hawaii, sinking most of the US Pacific Fleet and killing more than two thousand Americans—black and white, men and women, immigrants and native born. In a rousing speech to Congress, President Roosevelt called it "a date which will live in infamy."

It was also a day that set into motion the end of the Great Depression.

The United States immediately declared war against

The USS *Shaw* explodes during the Japanese surprise attack on Pearl Harbor on December 7, 1941.
National Archives and Records Administration

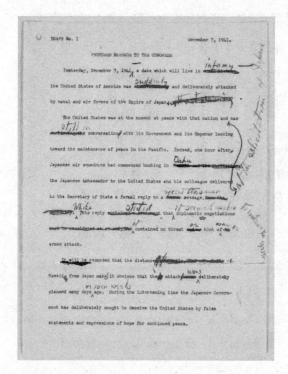

FDR's handwritten notes on his Pearl Harbor speech. A recording of the speech may be found at http://www.archives.gov/exhibits/american_originals/fdr.html.
Franklin D. Roosevelt Presidential Library and Museum

Japan. Germany and Italy—Japan's allies in the Axis—responded in turn by declaring war against the United States. In a matter of a few days, America had charged into World War II.

Hitler deceived himself into believing that a weakened United States would soon be defeated. "I don't see much future for the Americans," he commented, following the attack on Pearl Harbor.

America, however, was a sleeping giant. Since 1930, its citizens had stumbled forward in their search for a way out of the Great Depression. Now, faced with a mortal enemy and a threat to their safety and way of life, Americans were jolted into an awareness of their common destiny. It was no mere political slogan when FDR cheered on "American business, American labor, and American farmers, working together *as a patriotic team*" to defeat the Axis powers.

A man named Alan Lomax, working for the Library of Congress, traveled the country in the weeks after Pearl Harbor, hauling a large recording device. Lomax captured on tape the voices of ordinary people, creating a collection he called *After the Day of Infamy: "Man-on-the-Street" Interviews Following the Attack on Pearl Harbor*. At a moment of profound change in American history, Lomax listened to their shared fears, hopes, and determination:

> I think the time has come when we should all get behind our country. After all, we are all Americans and we should all be united against these dictator countries who are trying to invade our country and spoil our way of living. We are all Americans and I once more say, I am a hundred percent for President Roosevelt's speech.
>
> —FRANK TATREY

> We all are brothers. Let us remain brothers, don't care what creed are you or what color or who you are or where you come from. We all are American and let's fight for America and our brothers that is outside. Let's die American. If we have to go on the battlefield, let's die American.
>
> —ANONYMOUS INTERVIEWEE, PHILADELPHIA, PENNSYLVANIA

FDR and his advisers knew exactly what the United States needed to do to defeat its enemies overseas. The government, in Roosevelt's words, made the switch from "Doctor New Deal" to "Doctor Win-the-War."

The US government quickly became the nation's biggest shopper, spending billions of dollars on planes, bullets, food, uniforms, ships, and countless other items needed to defeat the Axis. By 1943, two years after Pearl Harbor, the government's purchases for the war effort amounted to over 40 percent of the entire US economy. Here are just some of the things the US government purchased from American manufacturers between 1942 and 1945: 310,000 aircraft, 10 battleships, 110,000 tanks and armored vehicles, 211 submarines, 12.5 million rifles, 806,073 2.5-ton trucks, 500 million socks, and 250 million pairs of pants.

An assembly line in 1942 at Ford's Willow Run plant—one of the largest factories in the world—where B-24 Liberator bombers were manufactured at the rate of one *per hour*.
Howard R. Hollem, photographer, Library of Congress, Office of War Information Collection

After the attack on Pearl Harbor, America assembled one of the largest war machines in the history of the world. Facing the armies of fascist Italy, Nazi Germany, and Imperial Japan, America became an unstoppable force. From 1941 to 1945, more than sixteen million American men and women served in the military as soldiers, sailors, pilots, nurses, and medics, and in thousands of other crucially important positions. For many of these people, military service was the first regular job they had ever held.

To fill the government's massive orders, Ford, General Motors,

A crew standing in front of an M4 Sherman tank at Fort Knox, Kentucky, during training in 1942.
Alfred T. Palmer, photographer, Library of Congress, Office of War Information Collection

US Steel, Boeing, and other companies brought dormant factories back to life and built thousands of new ones. Word went out to hire millions of new workers. Suddenly, formerly unemployed Americans were on the move, swarming the reborn factory towns and cities. Richmond, California, once a sleepy town of just twenty thousand

Women leaving after their shift at a uranium-enrichment plant in Oak Ridge, Tennessee. More than 80,000 people worked there. The secret race to build a nuclear weapon (called the Manhattan Project) created a mini–job boom for scientists, engineers, and others all over the country. The Manhattan Project ultimately hired 130,000 people, more than the population of most cities at the time, to research, design, and build the two atomic bombs that the United States would drop on the Japanese cities of Hiroshima and Nagasaki in 1945.
Ed Westcott, photographer, American Museum of Science and Energy Collection, 1944

residents, ballooned to more than one hundred thousand people—
many of them Dust Bowl refugees—who toiled at the gigantic Kaiser
Shipyards, which built a record 747 ships during the war. Once-rural
Texas became a state of giant industrial plants, from aircraft facto-
ries in Fort Worth to some of the world's largest fuel refineries, in
Beaumont and Port Arthur. Florida's population increased by nearly
50 percent, fueled by new shipyards in Jacksonville, Tampa, and
Pensacola.

All across the country, more jobs opened up than there were people to fill them. Wages skyrocketed for the first time in memory.

Military service and war industry jobs offered a giant boost to
Americans' health and morale. Lawrence Denton, who now worked
ten hours a day, six days a week at the Hanford nuclear reactor site
in Washington State, reflected on the "amazing experience for a man
from northern Idaho to come into a camp of fifty thousand people
going day and night." During the war years, as more people could once
again afford life's basic necessities, life expectancy—the number of
years a person was expected to live—increased by three years or more.

In 1943, unemployment in America dropped to its lowest point in
history—before or since. The US government's mobilization for war,
and its giant spending spree, had stopped the Depression in its tracks.

New energies released by the wartime economic boom super-
charged the whole society, bringing changes that had seemed impossible
only a few years earlier. In the late 1930s, Senator Robert LaFollette
Jr. had launched an investigation into what could be done to find a
permanent solution for California's migrant laborers. By 1942, the

Many new jobs also came with a cherished benefit: housing. In just one example, the Kaiser Shipyards in Portland, Oregon, helped construct Vanport, the nation's largest housing development built during the war—home to nearly ten thousand apartments and more than forty thousand residents, making it the second-largest city in the state. In this photograph, children and teachers play outside of a child care center in Vanport, in 1944.
City of Portland Archives and Records Center

question was moot: Nearly all of them had been hired by the airplane and munitions factories in Los Angeles and San Francisco. Now California's biggest problem was a migrant labor *shortage*. In response, in 1942 the United States created the Bracero Program, which admitted Mexican men into the country to work legally as agricultural laborers—reversing almost two decades of immigration restrictions.

Few changes to the workforce so astonished Americans as the

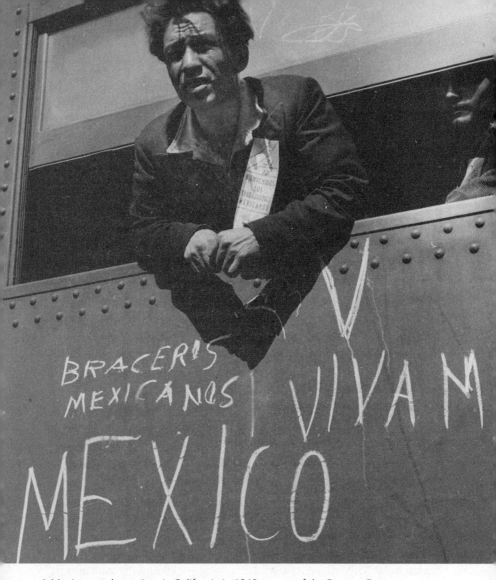

A Mexican worker arrives in California in 1942 as part of the Bracero Program.
Dorothea Lange, photographer. The Dorothea Lange Collection, Oakland Museum of California. Gift of Paul S. Taylor.
A67.137.42042.7

recruitment of women into jobs that had once been restricted to men. More than six and a half million women lined up to work as welders, riveters, and assembly line workers in aircraft factories, shipyards, and other companies turning out products for the war

A wartime recruitment poster aimed at persuading women to sign up for factory work. This image, along with others like it, became known as "Rosie the Riveter," an iconic character who represented and celebrated the millions of women who took on industrial jobs during World War II.
National Archives and Records Administration

effort. At Boeing, the giant aircraft manufacturer in Seattle, nearly half of the company's fifty thousand employees were women.

Cities such as Seattle, Portland, San Francisco, and Los Angeles swelled with the arrival of new women migrants looking for work. "In one month," Doris Eason of Seattle remembered, "we took applications from war workers from thirty-eight states... we had people from everywhere—from Montana and Idaho and Minnesota, and a number from different states in the South." Anne Wells, who worked at Boeing, recalled being "very proud to be there, to be a Rosie. I felt like I was doing my part and we all felt that way. It was a very serious business. The war began a major change on how women were seen, and how they saw themselves."

Grasping the importance of these sudden changes, Eleanor Roosevelt stepped in as a passionate advocate for women's equality at work, advocating (not always successfully) for equal pay and fair treatment for women on the job.

A worker riveting the wing of a B-24 Liberator bomber, at the Consolidated Aircraft Corporation, in Fort Worth, Texas, in 1944.
Howard R. Hollem, photographer, Library of Congress, Office of War Information Collection

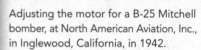

Adjusting the motor for a B-25 Mitchell bomber, at North American Aviation, Inc., in Inglewood, California, in 1942.
Alfred T. Palmer, photographer, Library of Congress, Office of War Information Collection

Assembling the SS *George Washington Carver* in Richmond, California, in 1943.
Schomburg Center for Research in Black Culture, Photographs and Prints Division, New York Public Library

The war also sparked radical changes in the lives of African Americans. Black men and women reported for military duty in numbers not seen since the Civil War. Detroit, Chicago, Los Angeles, Seattle, and other industrial centers across the country saw their black communities grow even larger, as 1.2 million African American people migrated to the North and West for defense jobs.

African Americans became vital to the war effort. This photograph shows Claude Mann, a driver in an M4 Sherman tank, near Nancy, France.
National Archives and Records Administration

Throughout the war years, most African American soldiers and workers found themselves shunted into menial and low-paying work, and exposed to the open racism of other soldiers, officers, and employers. Mob attacks on black workers, and even black soldiers and sailors, were commonplace. The military itself remained formally segregated until 1948, when President Harry S. Truman ordered its full integration.

In response, a new rallying cry echoed across African American communities: "Victory over our enemies at home and victory over our enemies on the battlefields abroad." The quiet struggle for rights

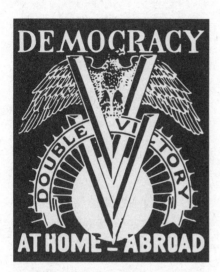

The *Pittsburgh Courier*, an African American newspaper, broadcast a call for "double victory."
Pittsburgh Courier

The Tuskegee Airmen, a celebrated squadron of African American fighter pilots, in 1939.
Schomburg Center for Research in Black Culture, Photographs and Prints Division, New York Public Library

that had simmered during the Great Depression broke into open militancy during World War II. Under Walter White's leadership, membership in the NAACP increased tenfold during the early 1940s. NAACP lawyer Thurgood Marshall's description of the situation in Texas applied to the nation as a whole: "Negroes in Texas do not care whether they lose or not" he wrote. "They are going to fight until they are allowed to vote."

Finally, for all people who worked on the home front to ensure an Allied victory over the Axis, labor unions became key players on FDR's "patriotic team." In 1941, nine million people belonged to unions; by 1945, that number had jumped to fifteen million, the greatest increase ever in such a short time, outstripping even the CIO's accomplishments in the 1930s.

On May 8, 1945, American radios broadcast the news that Nazi Germany had surrendered. Just a few months later, on August 14, Japan finally surrendered as well, following the US nuclear attacks on the Japanese cities of Hiroshima and Nagasaki.

FDR did not live to see the victory. Barely a month earlier, on April 12, the president died of complications from a long illness, after guiding the nation through four years of world war. Because the truth about FDR's health had been largely hidden, his death shocked the nation. Hundreds of thousands of people, many in tears, lined the funeral route from Warm Springs, Georgia, where he died, to his home in Hyde Park, where he was buried.

Americans mourned FDR not only as the hero of World War II but as the leader who saved them from the Great Depression. One magazine reported that "nowhere was grief so open as in the poorest neighborhoods of New York," the state where Franklin had first staked his political career. "In Old St. Patrick's in the heart of the Italian district on the lower east side," the story continued, "bowed, shabby figures came and went and, by the day after the President died, hundreds of candles burned in front of the altar. 'Never,' said a priest, 'have so many candles burned in this church.'"

A poster created during World War II, encouraging cooperation between workers and management at General Motors.
Smithsonian Institution, National Museum of American History

It concluded, "A woman clasped her 8-year-old son and said: 'Not in my lifetime or in yours will we again see such a man.'"

America's military victories set off celebrations of the sort that had not been seen or felt since the heyday of the Roaring Twenties.

A quieter but no less momentous victory had been won as well—this one on the home front. The US mainland had mostly escaped physical damage during the war, and the nation hummed with the energy of an economy in high gear. As American troops demobilized and returned home to their families, it was clear to many that a new world had taken shape—and that the experiments of the 1930s had hardened into a stable foundation.

Unlike nearly every other country on earth, America emerged from World War II stronger, more stable, and more unified than when it had begun.

Americans had defeated the Great Depression, at last.

ACKNOWLEDGMENTS

This book was nurtured, in different forms and over many years, by my wife, Patty, and by my two sons, Owen and Emmett. I wrote it for them, and with them always in mind. I might never have taken the leap toward the actual book without the guidance of Tanya McKinnon, my agent. I will always credit Tanya with the push I needed to make this happen. I am so grateful that Lisa Yoskowitz at Little, Brown Books for Young Readers was at the receiving end of the proposal. Her initial enthusiasm for the project—followed by round upon round of insightful and brilliant editing—buoyed my writing spirits and steered me well. Lisa's colleague Farrin Jacobs provided essential input at a key moment. Other members of the LBYR team, including Hallie Tibbetts, Hannah Milton, David Koral, Jen Graham, and Karina Granda, made an ungainly manuscript into a beautiful book. My hearty thanks goes out to all of them.

SOURCE NOTES

PART ONE: FALL

xvii   "We lived in a shack by the railroad tracks in Phoenix": Interview with William Wight, "Always Lending a Helping Hand," an oral history project documenting the Depression-era experiences of farming families in Sevier County, Utah, http://newdeal.feri.org/sevier/interviews.

CHAPTER ONE: DYSTOPIA, USA

4   "I remember the paperboys screaming about the stock market crash": Interview with James M. Franco, San Diego State University Oral History Project, 1973, http://library.sdsu.edu/scua/raising-our-voices/san-diego-history/great-depression.

6   "went hunting almost every day for food": Interview with Virginia Davis-Brown, "Providing for the Family During the Great Depression," Ypsilanti Historical Society, Spring 2016, http://ypsigleanings.aadl.org/node/356483.

6   "You must be rich": Interview with Violet Krall in Lucy Rogers Watkins, ed., *A Generation Speaks: Voices of the Great Depression* (Chapel Hill, NC: Chapel Hill Press, 2000), pp. 253–54.

6   "I didn't have the food I should have when I was carrying her": Interview with Vera Ruth Woodall Criswell, in "California Odyssey: The 1930s Migration to the Southern San Joaquin Valley," California State College–Bakersfield Oral History Program, 1981, http://www.csub.edu/library/_files/DB_files/Criswell114.pdf.

7   "We all got pretty low on food here": Coney (a farmer in England, Arkansas), quoted in *The New Republic*, May 27, 1931.

10   "You don't know what the heat is like in the Southwest": Interview with Stella Dean, "American Life Histories: Manuscripts from the Federal Writers' Project," Library of Congress, 1939, https://www.loc.gov/item/wpalh001838.

10   "a man and a woman and seven children lived in a hole in the ground": Interview with Mary Owsley in Studs Terkel, *Hard Times: An Oral History of the Great Depression* (New York: The New Press, 2005), p. 45.

13   "Slept in a paper box": "Blink," quoted in T. H. Watkins, *The Great Depression: America in the 1930s* (New York: Little, Brown and Company, 1993), p. 60.

15   "really began at the bottom": Interview with W. W. Tarver, "American Life Histories: Manuscripts from the Federal Writers' Project," Library of Congress, 1940, https://www.loc.gov/item/wpalh000498/.

18   "Thrifty Uncle Otis became destitute with the turn of the examiner's key": Dempsey Travis, quoted in Lizabeth Cohen, *Making a New Deal: Industrial Workers in Chicago, 1919–1939* (New York: Cambridge University Press, 2008), p. 215.

20   "Things remain at a standstill": Benjamin Roth, *The Great Depression: A Diary* (New York: PublicAffairs, 2009), pp. 40–41.

CHAPTER TWO: THE UNLUCKIEST PRESIDENT

23   "Hoover is certainly a wonder": FDR, quoted in Jean Edward Smith, *FDR* (New York: Random House, 2008), p. 177.

24   "was always hungry then": Herbert Hoover, quoted in William E. Leuchtenberg, *Herbert Hoover* (New York: Times Books, 2009), p. 3.

24   "put his teeth together with great decision.": Ibid., p. 6.

25   "the greatest humanitarian undertaking the world had ever seen": George H. Nash, *The Life of Herbert Hoover, the Humanitarian, 1914–1917* (New York: W. W. Norton & Company, 1988), p. 149.

26   "I have no dread of the ordinary work of the presidency": Herbert Hoover, quoted in Martin L. Fousold and George T. Mazuzan, eds., *The Hoover Presidency: A Reappraisal* (Albany: State University of New York Press, 1974), p. 52.

28   "They have preserved the American people from certain chaos": Herbert
      Hoover, address, October 22, 1932, Detroit, Michigan.

28   "If someone bit an apple": Will Rogers, quoted in "The Ordeal of Herbert
      Hoover, Part Two", *Prologue* 36, no. 2 (Summer 2004), https://www.archives
      .gov/publications/prologue/2004/summer/hoover-2.html.

31   "there is throughout the country a stirring among the unemployed": *The
      Nation*, May 29, 1932.

35   "Veterans were packing and rushing about.": Elbridge Purdy, quoted in Paul
      Dickson and Thomas B. Allen, *The Bonus Army: An American Epic* (New
      York: Walker & Company, 2004), p. 181.

36   "In order to put an end to this rioting and defiance of civil authority": Her-
      bert Hoover, "Statement About the Bonus Marchers," July 29, 1932.

37   "Every drop of blood shed today...can be laid directly on the threshold of the
      White House": Walter Waters, quoted in *The Nation*, July 27, 1932.

38   "must be extended by Government, not as a matter of charity": FDR, quoted
      in Arthur M. Schlesinger, *The Age of Roosevelt: The Crisis of the Old Order,
      1919–1933* (New York: Houghton Mifflin Harcourt, 2004), p. 392.

PART TWO: RISE

43   "I found a common understanding and unselfishness I'd never known": Vio-
      let Baggett, quoted in Priscilla Murolo and A. B. Chitty, *From the Folks Who
      Brought You the Weekend: A Short Illustrated History of Labor in the United
      States* (New York: The New Press, 2003), p. 212.

CHAPTER THREE: IT TAKES TWO

45   "I never saw him, but I knew him": Carl Carmer, quoted in Russell D. Buhite
      and David W. Levy, eds., *FDR's Fireside Chats* (Norman: University of Okla-
      homa Press, 1992), p. xx.

45   "A smile in the White House again seemed like a meal to us": Will Rogers,

quoted in Adam Cohen, *Nothing to Fear: FDR's Inner Circle and the Hundred Days That Created Modern America* (New York: The Penguin Press, 2009), p. 47.

46   "Eleanor Roosevelt set a new pace, new goals, a new understanding of what was possible": Blanche Wiesen Cook, introduction to Stephen Drury Smith, ed., *The First Lady of Radio: Eleanor Roosevelt's Historic Broadcasts* (New York: The New Press, 2014), p. 4.

47   "You have no looks, so see to it that you have manners": Anna Roosevelt, quoted in Blanche Wiesen Cook, *Eleanor Roosevelt*, vol. 1, *The Early Years, 1884–1933* (New York: Penguin Books, 1993), p. 62.

48   "Very early, I became conscious of the fact that there were people around me who suffered in one way or another": Eleanor Roosevelt, *The Autobiography of Eleanor Roosevelt* (New York: Harper Perennial, 2014), p. 12.

50   "he took a satisfaction in the purely political side of the struggle, in achieving new office.": Ibid., p. 153.

52   "Women must get into the political game, and stay in it": Eleanor Roosevelt, quoted in Blanche Wiesen Cook, *Eleanor Roosevelt*, vol. 1, *The Early Years, 1884–1933*, p. 393.

53   "It is common sense to take a method and try it: If it fails, admit it frankly and try another": FDR, speech at Oglethorpe University, May 22, 1932.

54   Marie Hurley, letter sourced from the American RadioWorks, "The First Family of Radio: Franklin and Eleanor Roosevelt's Historic Broadcasts," http://www.americanradioworks.org/documentaries/roosevelts.

56   "There was no kind of disturbance": Eleanor Roosevelt, quoted in Blanche Wiesen Cook, *Eleanor Roosevelt*, vol. 2, *The Defining Years, 1933–1938* (New York: Penguin Books, 2000), p. 46.

CHAPTER FOUR: PUSHING BACK

60   "seemed to have been dipped in phosphorus": Lillian Gish, quoted in Michael E. Parrish, *Anxious Decades: America in Prosperity and Depression, 1920–1941* (New York: W. W. Norton & Company, 1992), p. 289.

60   "Any man who can talk like that in times like these.": Sarah Love, quoted in David W. Houck, *FDR and Fear Itself: The First Inaugural Address* (College Station: Texas A&M Press, 2002), p. 10.

64   "the third great revolution in American history": Adam Cohen, *Nothing to Fear: FDR's Inner Circle and the Hundred Days That Created Modern America* (New York: The Penguin Press, 2009), p. 11.

64   "everybody was helping everybody": Interview with Madelyn Davidson, January 7, 1988, "Green Mountain Chronicles," Vermont Historical Society, https://vermonthistory.org/documents/GrnMtnChron Transcripts/199-20DavidsonMadelyn.pdf.

65   "Ten dollars a week, twelve hours a day": Interview with James M. Franco, San Diego State University Oral History Project, 1973, http://library.sdsu .edu/scua/raising-our-voices/san-diego-history/great-depression.

66   "it was the most rapid large-scale mobilization of men the country had ever witnessed": Robert Fechner, quoted in Christine Pfaff, "'Happy Days' of the Depression: The Civilian Conservation Corps in Colorado," *Colorado Heritage* (Spring 2001).

67   "If it had not been for the CCC, I don't know how [we] would have survived.": Interview with Carroll Burnette, "Civilian Conservation Corps Oral History Program," Samuel Proctor Oral History Program, University of Florida, February 8, 1999 interview, p. 14.

71–72   Carbon Hill quotations appear in "A New Deal for Carbon Hill, Alabama," by the New Deal Network, drawing on original documents in the WPA collection at the National Archives and Records Administration, http://newdeal .feri.org/carbonhill.

CHAPTER FIVE: THE REVOLUTIONARY

76   "I am now 72 years old and have never had anything": "Mrs. A.A. letter," from Eleanor Roosevelt Papers, Box 612, Franklin D. Roosevelt Presidential Library and Museum. Quoted in Robert. S. McElvaine, ed., *Down & Out in the Great Depression: Letters from the Forgotten Man*, Twenty-Fifth Anniversary Edition (Chapel Hill: University of North Carolina Press, 2008), p. 105.

79   "I had to do something about unnecessary hazards to life": Frances Perkins Oral History, Columbia University Libraries Oral History Research Office, p. 270.

80   "I was walking through Washington Square when a puff of smoke issuing from the factory building caught my eye": William Shepherd, *Milwaukee Journal*, March 27, 1911.

84   "I've been thinking things over and I've decided I want you to be secretary of labor": FDR, quoted in Frances Perkins, *The Roosevelt I Knew* (New York: Penguin Classics, 2011), p. 144.

86   "I said that if I accepted the position of Secretary of Labor I should want to do a great deal": Ibid., p. 145.

86   "You care about this thing": Ibid., p. 269.

89   "We can never insure one hundred percent of the population against one hundred percent of the hazards and vicissitudes of life": FDR's statement on signing the Social Security Act, August 14, 1935, quoted in the United States Social Security Administration website, "Social Security History," https://www.ssa.gov/history/fdrsignstate.html.

92   "I come from an old American family who pioneered this country": A.B. letter, Federal Emergency Relief Administration (FERA) New Subject File 002, quoted in Robert. S. McElvaine, p. 195.

CHAPTER SIX: A NEW WORLD

95   "It was a ten-hour workday": Interview with Marianna Costa, August 10, 1994, Library of Congress, American Folklife Center, Working in Paterson Project Collection, Folder 47, Box 2, WIP-DT-A010, A011.

95   "That water fountain wasn't over ten feet from me": Interview with Russell Gage, University of Michigan—Flint Labor History Project.

96   "We couldn't call our souls our own": Pennsylvania steelworker, quoted in Nelson Lichtenstein, *State of the Union: A Century of American Labor* (Princeton, NJ: Princeton University Press, 2012), p. 31.

96   "We work in *his* mine": West Virginia coal miner, quoted in Michael E.

Parrish, *Anxious Decades: America in Prosperity and Depression, 1920–1941* (New York: W. W. Norton & Company, 1992), p. 289.

100 "they are union mad": Government official, quoted in Kathryn S. Olmsted, *Right Out of California: The 1930s and the Big Business Roots of Modern Conservatism* (New York: The New Press, 2015), p. 41.

103 "The foreman was pretty well astonished": Interview with Bob Stinson in Studs Terkel, *Hard Times: An Oral History of the Great Depression* (New York: The New Press, 2005), p. 130.

105 "Gather round me and I'll tell you all a story": A song recorded by Alan Lomax, Library of Congress, American Folklife Center, John A. Lomax and Alan Lomax Papers, Folder 420, AFC 1933/001.

105–6 "I shall personally enter General Motors": John L. Lewis, quoted in Murray Kempton, *Part of Our Time: Some Ruins and Monuments of the Thirties* (New York: NYRB Classics, 2004), p. 60.

107 "CIO, CIO": A song recorded by Ida and William Rinas during the strike, quoted in an interview with Ida and William Rinas, in "American Life Histories: Manuscripts from the Federal Writers' Project, 1936–1940," https://www.loc.gov/item/wpalh000079.

110 "not only the curse of the working man in this country": John Sargent, quoted in Lizabeth Cohen, *Making a New Deal: Industrial Workers in Chicago, 1919–1939* (New York: Cambridge University Press, 2009), p. 293.

111 "We accomplished union representation": Interview with Marianna Costa.

PART THREE: SETBACK

113 "It was as though the sky was divided into two opposite worlds": Pauline Winkler Grey, quoted in "The Black Sunday of April 14, 1935," collected in "Pioneer Stories of Meade County, Meade County (Kansas) Council of Women's Clubs, 1950."

CHAPTER SEVEN: DARK CLOUDS

116   "On Sunday in April, 1935, and I was grading papers": Interview with Lola Adams Crum, June 23, 1998, Ford County Dust Bowl Oral History Project. Ford County Historical Society: A Kansas Humanities Council Funded Project. Dodge City, Kansas.

116   "The dust drifted like snow": Winton Slagle Sipe, "Memories of a Kansas Farm Boy. Part Six: Dust Bowl Days," the Kansas Collection, www.kancoll.org.

117   "My dad had a sale and we sold everything we owned": Interview with Ethel Oleta Wever Belezzuoli, in "California Odyssey: The 1930s Migration to the Southern San Joaquin Valley," California State College–Bakersfield Oral History Program, 1981, http://www.csub.edu/library//_files/DB_files/Belezzuoli124.pdf.

118   "a big twelve-cylinder Nash, one car packed with ten people": Interview with Oscar Ervin Kludt, "California Odyssey: The 1930s Migration to the Southern San Joaquin Valley," http://www.csub.edu/library//_files/DB_files/Kludt134.pdf.

120   "We didn't realize there were so many people on the road": Interview with Vera Ruth Woodall Criswell, in "California Odyssey: The 1930s Migration to the Southern San Joaquin Valley," http://www.csub.edu/library/_files/DB_files/Criswell114.pdf.

121   "would camp at night and build little fires and do our cooking": Interview with Loye Lucille Martin Holmes interview, in "California Odyssey: The 1930s Migration to the Southern San Joaquin Valley," http://www.csub.edu/library/_files/DB_files/Holmes113.pdf.

121   "When they need us they call us migrants": Quoted in John Steinbeck's "The Harvest Gypsies, Part I," *San Francisco News*, October 5–12, 1936.

121   "filth, squalor, and entire absence of sanitation": Government investigator, quoted in Kathryn S. Olmsted, *Right Out of California: The 1930s and the Big Business Roots of Modern Conservatism* (New York: The New Press, 2015), p. 123.

123   "I'd Rather Not Be on Relief": Song recorded in the Shafter FSA camp, California, 1938, Library of Congress, American Folklife Center, Voices from the Dust Bowl: The Charles L. Todd and Robert Sonkin Migrant Worker Collection.

123   "We would find either side of the highway just dotted with these old, beat-up cars": Interview with Juliet Thorner, M.D., in "California Odyssey: the 1930s Migration to the Southern San Joaquin Valley."

124   "She told me her age, that she was thirty-two": Dorothea Lange, quoted in *Popular Photography*, February 1960.

126   "The look of hunger was already in the camp": Roger Sprague quoted in Linda Gordon, *Dorothea Lange: A Life Beyond Limits* (New York: W. W. Norton & Company, 2009), p. 237.

126–27 "When the ranch dried up and blew away": John Steinbeck, "The Harvest Gypsies," *San Francisco News*, October 5–12, 1936.

CHAPTER EIGHT: THE BLIND SPOT

131   "just wanted you to stay": Lillie Fenner, quoted in William Chafe, Ray Gavins, and Robert Korstad, eds., *Remembering Jim Crow: African Americans Tell About Life in the Segregated South* (New York: The New Press, 2001), p. 235.

137   "I knew if a white woman": Quoted in James Goodman, *Stories of Scottsboro* (New York: Vintage, 2013), p. 3.

139   "every Negro in the country.": Charles Hamilton Houston, quoted in Patricia Sullivan, *Lift Every Voice: The NAACP and the Making of the Civil Rights Movement* (New York, The New Press, 2009), p. 162.

139   "if I have to spend more than one or two years longer": Roy Wright, quoted in "Scottsboro: An American Tragedy," http://www.pbs.org/wgbh//amex/scottsboro/peopleevents/p_lwright.html.

144   "to all of those who have spoken to me about it, I have urged patience": Walter White, letter to Eleanor Roosevelt, January 10, 1935, Franklin D. Roosevelt Presidential Library and Museum, http://www.fdrlibrary.marist.edu/_resources/images/ersel/ersel098b.pdf.

CHAPTER NINE: ENEMIES

147   "I hope that Wall St will never have the power again": Anonymous letter, from the National Archives, President's Emergency Committee on Employment files, 003, Tray I-1; quoted in Robert. S. McElvaine, ed. *Down & Out in the Great Depression: Letters from the Forgotten Man*, Twenty-Fifth Anniversary Edition (Chapel Hill: University of North Carolina Press, 2008), p. 42.

149   "operating all over this country shaking down immigrants.": Frances Perkins Oral History, Columbia University Libraries Oral History Research Office, p. 240.

150   "the day of judgment": Woman quoted in Francisco E. Balderrama and Raymond Rodriguez, *Decade of Betrayal: Mexican Repatriation in the 1930s* (Albuquerque: University of New Mexico Press, 2006), p. 71.

150   "by the truckload—men, women, and children—with dogs, cats, and goats... half-open suitcases, rolls of bedding, and lunch baskets": Carey McWilliams, quoted in Francisco E. Balderrama and Raymond Rodriguez, p. 130.

151   "My family lived in Erie [Colorado] and my father had taken me along to shop in Longmont.": Emma Gomez Martinez, quoted in the Boulder County Latino History Project, BCLHP-FP-051, http://bocolatinohistory.colorado.edu/document/mexican-deportation-in-the-1930s-by-emma-gomez-martinez.

152   "the most useful citizen of the United Stated politically": Quoted in Alan Brinkley, *Voices of Protest: Huey Long, Father Coughlin, and the Great Depression* (New York: Vintage, 1983), p. 120.

152   "He said he would rely on me": Father Charles Coughlin, ibid., p. 125.

157   "You know, we always cling to the hope something is going to happen.": Interview with Gerda Blachmann Wilchfort, for the United States Holocaust Memorial Museum online exhibit on the voyage of the *St. Louis*, https://www.ushmm.org/wlc/en/article.php?ModuleId=10005267.

PART FOUR: VICTORY

CHAPTER TEN: A WAR TO DEFEAT THE DEPRESSION

164 "I don't see much future for the Americans": Adolf Hitler, quoted in David M. Kennedy, *Freedom from Fear: The American People in Depression and War, 1929–1945* (New York: Oxford University Press, 2005), p. 615.

164–65 "American business, American labor, and American farmers, working together as a patriotic team": FDR, Navy Day Speech, October 27, 1944.

169 "amazing experience for a man from northern Idaho to come into a camp of fifty thousand people going day and night": Interview with Lawrence Denton by Cynthia Kelly and Tom Zannes, "Voices of the Manhattan Project," Atomic Heritage Foundation, Hanford, WA, September 2003, http://manhattanprojectvoices.org/oral-histories/lawrence-dentons-interview.

172 "In one month we took applications from war workers from thirty-eight states"; "I felt like I was doing my part and we all felt that way.": Doris Eason and Anne Wells, quoted in http://features.crosscut.com/seattles-working-women-of-world-war-ii-an-oral-history.

175 "Negroes in Texas do not care whether they lose or not": Thurgood Marshall, quoted in Patricia Sullivan, *Lift Every Voice: The NAACP and the Making of the Civil Rights Movement* (New York: The New Press, 2009), p. 246.

176 "nowhere was grief so open as in the poorest neighborhoods of New York": from *Yank Magazine*, quoted in Gabe Pressman, "The Day FDR Died," http://www.nbcnewyork.com/news/local/The-Day-FDR-Died-119716909.html, April 12, 2011.

BIBLIOGRAPHY

Badger, Anthony. *The New Deal: The Depression Years, 1933–1940*. Chicago: Ivan R. Dee, 1989.

Balderrama, Francisco E., and Raymond Rodriguez. *Decade of Betrayal: Mexican Repatriation in the 1930s*. Albuquerque: University of New Mexico Press, 2006.

Bernstein, Irving. *The Turbulent Years: A History of the American Worker, 1933–1940*. Chicago: Haymarket Books, 2010.

Brinkley, Alan. *Voices of Protest: Huey Long, Father Coughlin, and the Great Depression*. New York: Vintage, 1983.

Cohen, Adam. *Nothing to Fear: FDR's Inner Circle and the Hundred Days That Created Modern America*. New York: The Penguin Press, 2009.

Cohen, Lizabeth. *Making a New Deal: Industrial Workers in Chicago, 1919–1939*. New York: Cambridge University Press, 2009.

Cook, Blanche Wiesen. *Eleanor Roosevelt*. Vol.1, *The Early Years, 1884–1933*. New York: Penguin Books, 1993.

———. *Eleanor Roosevelt*. Vol. 2, *The Defining Years, 1933–1938*. New York: Penguin Books, 2000.

Dickson, Paul, and Thomas B. Allen. *The Bonus Army: An American Epic*. New York: Walker & Company, 2004.

Downey, Kirstin. *The Woman Behind the New Deal: The Life and Legacy of Frances Perkins, Social Security, Unemployment Insurance, and the Minimum Wage*. New York: Anchor, 2010.

Dubovsky, Melvyn, and Warren Van Tine. *John L. Lewis: A Biography*. Chicago: University of Illinois Press, 1986.

Egan, Timothy. *The Worst Hard Time: The Untold Story of Those Who Survived the Great American Dust Bowl*. New York: Houghton Mifflin, 2006.

Fine, Sidney. *Sit Down: The General Motors Strike of 1936–1937*. Ann Arbor: University of Michigan Press, 1969.

Foner, Eric. "The New Deal and the Redefinition of Freedom." Chap. 9 in *The Story of American Freedom*. New York: W. W. Norton & Company, 1999.

Freedman, Russell. *Children of the Great Depression*. New York: HMH Books for Young Readers, 2010.

Galbraith, John Kenneth. *The Great Crash 1929*. New York: Mariner Books, 2010.

Gerstle, Gary. *American Crucible: Race and Nation in the Twentieth Century*. Princeton, NJ: Princeton University Press, 2017.

Goodman, James. *Stories of Scottsboro*. New York: Vintage, 2013.

Gordon, Linda. *Dorothea Lange: A Life Beyond Limits*. New York: W. W. Norton & Company, 2009.

Hiltzik, Michael. *The New Deal: A Modern History*. New York: Free Press, 2011.

James, Rawn, Jr. *Double V: How Wars, Protest, and Harry Truman Desegregated America's Military*. New York: Bloomsbury, 2013.

Janken, Kenneth Robert. *White: The Biography of Walter White, Mr. NAACP*. New York: The New Press, 2003.

Katznelson, Ira. *Fear Itself: The New Deal and the Origins of Our Time*. New York: W. W. Norton & Company, 2013.

Kennedy, David M. *Freedom from Fear: The American People in Depression and War, 1929–1945*. New York: Oxford University Press, 2005.

Kyvig, David E. *Daily Life in the United States, 1920–1940: How Americans Lived Through the "Roaring Twenties" and the Great Depression*. Chicago: Ivan R. Dee, 2004.

Lash, Joseph P. *Eleanor and Franklin*. New York: W. W. Norton & Company, 2014.

Leuchtenberg, William E. *Franklin D. Roosevelt and the New Deal, 1932–1940*. New York: Harper Perennial, 2009.

———. *Herbert Hoover*. New York: Times Books, 2009.

Lowitt, Richard, and Maurine Beasley, eds. *One Third of Nation: Lorena Hickock Reports on the Great Depression*. Chicago: University of Illinois Press, 2000.

McElvaine, Robert S., ed. *Down & Out in the Great Depression: Letters from the Forgotten Man*, Twenty-Fifth Anniversary Edition. Chapel Hill: University of North Carolina Press, 2008.

Nash, George H. *The Life of Herbert Hoover, the Humanitarian, 1914–1917*. New York: W. W. Norton & Company, 1988.

Ngai, Mae. *Impossible Subjects: Illegal Aliens and the Making of Modern America*. Princeton, NJ: Princeton University Press, 2004.

Olmsted, Kathryn S. *Right Out of California: The 1930s and the Big Business Roots of Modern Conservatism*. New York: The New Press, 2015.

Parrish, Michael E. *Anxious Decades: America in Prosperity and Depression, 1920–1941*. New York: W. W. Norton & Company, 1992.

Perkins, Frances. *The Roosevelt I Knew*. New York: Penguin Classics, 2011.

Roosevelt, Eleanor. *The Autobiography of Eleanor Roosevelt*. New York: Harper Perennial, 2014.

Rosengarten, Theodore. *All God's Dangers: The Life of Nate Shaw*. Chicago: University of Chicago Press, 2000.

Roth, Benjamin, *The Great Depression: A Diary*. New York: PublicAffairs, 2009.

Schlesinger, Arthur M., *The Age of Roosevelt: The Crisis of the Old Order, 1919–1933*. New York: Houghton Mifflin Harcourt, 2004.

Smith, Stephen, ed. *The First Lady of Radio: Eleanor Roosevelt's Historic Broadcasts*. New York: The New Press, 2014.

Sullivan, Patricia. *Days of Hope: Race and Democracy in the New Deal Era*. Chapel Hill: University of North Carolina Press, 1996.

———. *Lift Every Voice: The NAACP and the Making of the Civil Rights Movement*. New York: The New Press, 2009.

Taylor, Nick. *American-Made: The Enduring Legacy of the WPA: When FDR Put the Nation to Work*. New York: Bantam, 2009.

Terkel, Studs. *Hard Times: An Oral History of the Great Depression*. New York: The New Press, 2005.

Watkins, T. H. *The Great Depression: America in the 1930s*. New York: Little, Brown and Company, 1993.

Wilkerson, Isabel. *The Warmth of Other Suns: The Epic Story of America's Great Migration*. New York: Vintage, 2011.

Worster, Donald. *Dust Bowl: The Southern Plains in the 1930s*. New York: Oxford University Press, 2004.

Ziegelman, Jane, and Andrew Coe. *A Square Meal: A Culinary History of the Great Depression*. New York: HarperCollins, 2016.

SELECTED PRIMARY SOURCES

You can explore the history of the Great Depression in different media, through many different collections of primary sources at libraries and archives across the country. I have included those that are accessible online, and that can be easily navigated by readers of all ages.

I. ONLINE MULTIMEDIA EXHIBITS

The Franklin D. Roosevelt Presidential Library and Museum houses a large collection of documents, photographs, and recordings relating to the life of FDR and Eleanor Roosevelt. Much of the material is accessible online.

https://fdrlibrary.org

"Frances Perkins: The Woman Behind the New Deal" is an online exhibit hosted by the Columbia University Libraries, which includes a full narrative of Perkins's life and work, with photographs and documents.

https://exhibitions.cul.columbia.edu/exhibits/show/perkins

The Herbert Hoover Presidential Library–Museum contains photographs, letters, information on his life and presidency, as well as the full text of his autobiography.

https://hoover.archives.gov

The New Deal Network is an online resource for information on New Deal public works and arts projects, including a major database of photographs, political cartoons, and texts.

http://newdeal.feri.org

The Living New Deal is an evolving national database that seeks to document the full extent of New Deal public works projects across the United States. It also includes extensive information about all the different New Deal agencies and their history.

https://livingnewdeal.org

"The History of Social Security" is a thorough and well-documented online resource for exploring the history of the Social Security Act of 1935 and its amendments in subsequent years, as well as the history of the US government's administration of Social Security from the New Deal to the present.

https://www.ssa.gov/history/index.html

The University of Detroit Mercy is the home of a large collection of primary source materials related to the career of Father Coughlin, including photographs, pamphlets, audio recordings of his speeches, and issues of *Social Justice*, the magazine he produced.

http://research.udmercy.edu/find/special_collections/digital/coughlin/index.php

The United States Holocaust Memorial Museum website hosts a major online exhibit on the voyage of the *St. Louis*.

https://www.ushmm.org/wlc/en/article.php?ModuleId=10005267

II. VISUAL SOURCES

Farm Security Administration/Office of War Information Photographs

Between 1935 and 1944, photographers working for the US government created a massive photographic record of life in the United States. The collection includes approximately 175,000 black-and-white images, and an additional 1,600 color photographs. The original negatives are housed at the Library of

Congress in Washington, DC. The photography project was first launched under the direction of the Farm Security Administration, a New Deal agency; during World War II, it was transferred to the Office of War Information.

The FSA/OWI photographs, as they are known, are a treasure trove of visual information about the daily experiences of Americans during the Great Depression. Many of the photographers who helped create this collection—including Dorothea Lange, Walker Evans, Ben Shahn, Gordon Parks, Jack Delano, and Russell Lee—are among the most celebrated American artists of the twentieth century.

The Library of Congress has made all of these photographs available online.

http://www.loc.gov/pictures/collection/fsa
http://www.loc.gov/pictures/collection/fsac

WPA Posters

Of the more than two thousand posters created by artists working for the WPA— which advertised a range of different government-sponsored programs—more than nine hundred can be found at the Library of Congress.

http://www.loc.gov/pictures/collection/wpapos

Painting and Other Visual Arts

Despite the immense financial pressures on all Americans, the upheaval of the Great Depression inspired visual artists to examine American life with fresh eyes. Beginning in 1934, the New Deal also supported many artists in their work, helping to create a kind of renaissance in American visual arts. The artists listed below are a sample of the most important creators during this time. Much of their work can be found in online exhibits or at fine arts museums across the country.

Thomas Hart Benton
Henry Billings
Harry Brodsky
Jacob Burck
Bernice Cross
Arthur Durston
Mabel Dwight
Seymour Fogel
Lily Furedi

Hugo Gellert
Charles L. Goeller
Blanche Grambs
William Gropper
Edward Hopper
Eli Jacobi
Alberta Kinsey
Louis Lozowick
Reginald Marsh
Edward Millman
Elizabeth Olds
Earle Richardson
Diego Rivera
James N. Rosenberg
Ben Shahn
Isaac Soyer
Raphael Soyer
Harry Sternberg
Prentiss Taylor
James Turnbull
Julius Weiss
Grant Wood

III. AUDIO SOURCES

Transcripts of all of Franklin Roosevelt's speeches and fireside chats are available online, courtesy of the FDR Presidential Library and Museum.

**http://www.fdrlibrary.marist.edu/archives/collections/franklin/index.php?p
=collections/findingaid&id=582**

An original audio recording of FDR's first inaugural address is available at the National Archives website.

https://archive.org/details/FranklinDelanoRooseveltfdrFearItself

"The First Family of Radio: Franklin and Eleanor Roosevelt's Historic Broadcasts" is a project of American RadioWorks, the documentary production arm of American Public Media. It includes an original radio documentary about the Roosevelts' use of radio, as well as other recordings; letters; and historical information about the Roosevelts during the Depression and World War II.

http://www.americanradioworks.org/documentaries/roosevelts

The Flint Sit-Down Strike Audio Gallery includes original audio interviews with participants in the 1936 strike.

http://flint.matrix.msu.edu/strike.php

This website at Michigan State University houses audio recordings of the interviews that formed the basis for Studs Terkel's *Hard Times: An Oral History of the Great Depression*.

http://studsterkel.matrix.msu.edu/htimes.php

"The Great Depression Interviews," at the Film and Media Archive at Washington University Libraries, are part of the Henry Hampton Collection, which were used in a seven-part PBS documentary.

http://digital.wustl.edu/greatdepression/index.html

"Voices from the Dust Bowl: The Charles L. Todd and Robert Sonkin Migrant Worker Collection" at the Library of Congress is an online exhibit of sound recordings (songs and spoken word) collected at migrant labor camps in California.

https://www.loc.gov/collections/todd-and-sonkin-migrant-workers-from-1940-to-1941

IV. PRINTED INTERVIEWS AND ORAL HISTORIES

"American Life Histories: Manuscripts from the Federal Writers Project, 1936–1940" is a collection that includes almost three thousand documents describing the lives of ordinary Americans during the Great Depression. They were collected by a team of three hundred writers hired by the government as part of a New Deal jobs program called the Folklore Project, which was part of the Federal Writers Project, under the Works Progress Administration (WPA).

https://www.loc.gov/collections/federal-writers-project/about-this-collection

"Always Lending a Helping Hand" is an oral history project documenting the Depression-era experiences of farming families in Sevier County, Utah.

http://newdeal.feri.org/sevier/interviews

"Behind The Veil: Documenting African American Life in the Jim Crow South" is a large collection of oral histories of black southerners during the segregation era, including many that describe life in the 1930s.

http://library.duke.edu/digitalcollections/behindtheveil

The Oral History Program of the California Odyssey Project at California State University–Bakersfield includes a broad range of interviews with people who made the Dust Bowl migration from Kansas, Oklahoma, Arkansas, and Texas to California.

http://www.csub.edu/library/SpecialCollection/Dustbowl/Interviews.html

The Ford County Historical Society in Kansas has recorded a number of interviews with Dust Bowl survivors in that area.

http://www.kansashistory.us/fordco/dustbowl

"Rosie the Riveter World War Two American Home Front Oral History project," at the Oral History Center of the Bancroft Library at the University of California–Berkeley is a large collection of original oral history interviews with Californians and others who lived through the massive wartime work mobilization during World War II.

http://bancroft.berkeley.edu/ROHO/projects/rosie

This article from Crosscut.com includes numerous first-person accounts of women from the Seattle area during World War II, many of whom went to work in the Boeing aircraft manufacturing plants.

http://features.crosscut.com/seattles-working-women-of-world-war-ii-an -oral-history

"Voices of the Manhattan Project" is a joint project of the Atomic Heritage Foundation and the Los Alamos Historical Society, which includes more than four hundred interviews with Manhattan Project workers and their families.

http://manhattanprojectvoices.org

TIMELINE OF THE GREAT DEPRESSION

OCTOBER 29, 1929:

"Black Tuesday," the US stock market collapses.

SPRING 1930:

Unemployment in the United States has doubled to more than three million people, since the Crash.

NOVEMBER 17, 1930:

The National Bank of Kentucky goes out of business, triggering a wave of bank runs and bank closures.

DECEMBER 11, 1930:

The Bank of the United States, the fourth-largest bank in New York City, collapses.

FEBRUARY 26, 1931:

Immigration officers in Los Angeles surround La Placita park and arrest more than four hundred Mexicans and Mexican Americans, part of a larger campaign to deport hundreds of thousands of people to Mexico during the Depression.

MARCH 25, 1931:

Nine African American men and boys are arrested in Alabama; the "Scottsboro Boys" trial becomes a national sensation.

SUMMER 1932:

The "Bonus Army" marches on Washington; tens of thousands of veterans and their families are violently evicted on July 28.

NOVEMBER 1932:

Franklin D. Roosevelt is elected president in a landslide victory over Herbert Hoover.

1933:

Unemployment in the United States reaches a high of 25 percent of the working-age population.

MARCH 4, 1933:

Roosevelt is inaugurated as president of the United States, and in his first inaugural address reassures Americans that "the only thing we have to fear is fear itself."

MARCH 6, 1933:

Roosevelt declares a four-day bank holiday to prevent further bank runs.

MARCH 9, 1933:

Congress passes the Emergency Banking Act, beginning the first "hundred days" of legislation aimed at stabilizing and reviving the US economy.

MARCH 12, 1933:

Roosevelt gives his first national radio address, or "fireside chat," which becomes a hallmark of his presidency.

FEBRUARY 23, 1934:

Senator Huey Long of Louisiana announces the creation of his "Share Our Wealth" plan on a national radio broadcast. Along with the Townsend Plan, this helps put pressure on President Roosevelt to establish a national system of Social Security.

FEBRUARY 1935:

The Costigan-Wagner Bill, which would have made lynching a federal crime, dies in the Senate when southern senators threaten to block it and President Roosevelt refuses to support it.

APRIL 14, 1935:

The "Black Sunday" dust storm rolls across the Great Plains, one of the largest storms of what becomes known as the "Dust Bowl."

JULY 1935:

President Roosevelt signs the National Labor Relations Act ("Wagner Act").

AUGUST 1935:

President Roosevelt signs the Social Security Act into law, creating the first strands of America's social safety net.

FEBRUARY OR MARCH 1936:

Dorothea Lange encounters Florence Owens Thompson and her children in a migrant camp in Nipomo, California; her *Migrant Mother* photograph of Owens becomes the iconic image of the Depression.

DECEMBER 30, 1936:

Workers at the General Motors plant in Flint, Michigan, stage a sit-down strike that will last forty-four days and end in victory for the United Automobile Workers union.

JUNE 25, 1938:

President Roosevelt signs into law the Fair Labor Standards Act, which outlaws child labor and establishes a national minimum wage, the forty-hour workweek, and overtime pay for certain jobs.

APRIL 14, 1939:

John Steinbeck's *The Grapes of Wrath* is published, quickly becoming the best-selling book of the Depression era.

1941:

On December 7, the Empire of Japan attacks Pearl Harbor.

1942:

Unemployment reaches its lowest point since 1930.

1944:

Unemployment reaches its lowest point in US history.

APRIL 12, 1945:

President Franklin Delano Roosevelt dies in Warm Springs, Georgia.

GREAT DEPRESSION GLOSSARY

Agricultural Adjustment Act: A key piece of the New Deal, which provided payments to farmers in exchange for harvesting fewer crops. Though its goal was to raise agricultural prices, the AAA also had the unintended consequence of causing thousands of black and white sharecroppers in the South to be evicted from plantations when plantation owners (who pocketed the government payments) reduced their cotton crop acreage.

Arkies: Migrants from Arkansas, who fled poverty conditions in that state in search of better lives and work in California.

bank holiday: A government-sanctioned (state or federal) closure of a bank for business to prevent a bank run.

bank run: A rush by most or all of the customers of a bank to withdraw their funds, out of fear that the institution may collapse.

Bonus Army: A loosely organized group of World War I veterans who traveled to Washington, DC, in the summer of 1932 to demand payment of a cash bonus promised to them by the federal government.

Civilian Conservation Corps: One of the earliest job-creation programs of the New Deal, employing hundreds of thousands of men at CCC camps across the country.

The Congress of Industrial Organizations: A new kind of labor union that sought to organize all workers—at all skill levels—within a given industry. The CIO was responsible for the enormous surge in union membership during the 1930s.

deportation: The forcible removal from the country, by the government, of a person who is not a citizen of the United States.

depression: A severe economic downturn or slump that lasts an extended period of time, and contributes to widespread unemployment.

Dust Bowl: An extended drought in the Great Plains states of Kansas, Oklahoma, Arkansas, and Texas in the 1930s that caused topsoil to blow away and created huge dust clouds across the middle part of the United States.

eviction: The forcible removal of a person or family from their home or property by the police, as the result of a court order. Evictions were widespread in communities across the United States during the Great Depression.

fireside chats: Radio speeches given by President Roosevelt throughout the 1930s and early 1940s, notable for their conversational and intimate tone.

foreclosure: When a bank or other financial lender takes back a home because the owner can no longer make mortgage payments.

hobo: A person who wanders the country in search of work.

Hooverville: A group of shacks, named after President Herbert Hoover, housing homeless people during the Great Depression.

hundred days: The first three months of Franklin Roosevelt's presidency, when many key pieces of New Deal legislation were passed, laws which fundamentally changed the role of the government in American life.

Jim Crow: The name given to the practice of segregation and racism in the American South before the civil rights movement.

layoffs: When workers lose their jobs because an employer is closing or no longer able or willing to pay them.

lynching: The murder, usually by a mob, of a person who has not been legally tried or convicted of a crime.

New Deal: A set of government programs, launched by President Franklin D. Roosevelt, that sought to reverse the effects of the Great Depression and also protect Americans from future economic downturns.

Okies: Migrants or refugees from the state of Oklahoma, which was hard hit by the Dust Bowl during the 1930s.

"repatriation": An effort by government officials and private citizens to persuade (or force) immigrants to return to their home countries.

Rosie the Riveter: The name given to women who went to work in the wartime industries (many of whom operated rivet guns at aircraft factors in California, Washington State, and Texas) during the Second World War.

Scottsboro Boys: A group of nine African American men and boys falsely accused of rape and arrested in Alabama in 1931; their trial attracted national attention.

scrip: Artificial currency that is used as a means of exchange, when official currency no longer has any value or is in short supply.

segregation: The practice of separating people on the basis of race, in housing, schools, and public facilities.

sharecropper: A kind of farmer who rents land in exchange for keeping a portion of his or her crop.

sit-down strike: A kind of strike in which workers occupy the factories they work in as a negotiation tactic with their employers—preventing a company from operating.

Social Security: A program created by President Roosevelt in 1935 that provided guaranteed retirement income for many American workers.

stock market crash: A sudden drop in stock prices that results from panic selling by investors.

Tennessee Valley Authority: A government-owned corporation created as part of the New Deal in May 1933. The TVA constructed dams, electrical power generators, and flood-control programs in seven states, as one of the largest public works projects in American history.

Townsend Plan: A plan developed during the Great Depression by Dr. Francis Townsend that called for every American over the age of sixty to be supported by government payments of $200 per month—funded by a 2 percent national sales tax. The Townsend Plan was enormously popular, and helped push President Roosevelt toward creating a national Social Security program in 1935.

tramp: A homeless person who wanders in search of free food and handouts.

unemployment: Lack of work, often due to an economic downturn.

union: An organization formed by workers who wish to act together to negotiate with their employers over wages, working conditions, or hours.

Works Progress Administration: The largest New Deal agency, created in May 1935. Headed by Harry Hopkins, the WPA employed millions of Americans during the Great Depression, putting them to work on arts, construction, and educational projects.

INDEX

Turn the page for a preview of

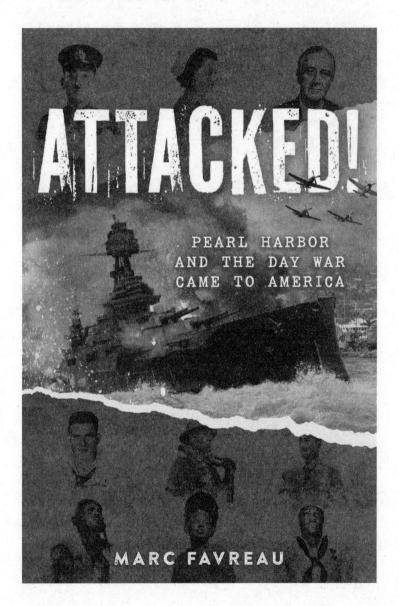

ATTACKED!

PEARL HARBOR
AND THE DAY WAR
CAME TO AMERICA

MARC FAVREAU

PROLOGUE
The Ghosts of History

PEARL HARBOR.

The first time I saw these two words, they were at the top of a dreaded pop quiz.

Our fifth-grade math teacher had scrawled them there, and we knew it meant something important—but what? She was growing impatient with how little attention we were paying to her latest lesson. The moment had come, she said, to see what we were made of.

We had no idea what "Pearl Harbor" meant. But for people of my math teacher's generation, I later learned, those two words needed no explaining. They were about the power of surprise, about treachery, and about how something could literally come out of the sky and change your world forever.

Their meaning had a flip side, too: that you must always be prepared.

I later learned that Pearl Harbor was where one of the most important events in all of American history had taken place. But I came to understand it was something more than that: Pearl Harbor was a history lesson, one that neither my teacher nor the America she was born into had ever recovered from. The world was a dangerous place, it said, filled with evil and uncertainty—and America always had to be ready for what came its way.

We had been given no warning that such a math quiz was coming. Were we prepared?

⎯⎯◇⎯⎯

On December 7, 1941, four decades before I was handed that math quiz, the Imperial Japanese Navy launched a devastating attack against the US Pacific Fleet, headquartered in Pearl Harbor, Oahu, one of the volcanic islands that make up Hawaii, at the time a US territory.

The United States of America was caught completely off guard. No one could remember anything like this happening before, and Americans vowed never to let it happen again. On street corners, at bus stops, in train stations and school hallways, the same message appeared: REMEMBER PEARL HARBOR.

Pearl Harbor jolted Americans awake. For years, Adolf Hitler's Nazi armies had been on the march across Europe. In 1940, Imperial Japan joined Hitler's "Axis" of dictatorships and was sweeping across Asia. Before Pearl Harbor, most Americans believed that they were safe—insulated from Europe and Asia by two oceans—and could choose when, where, or whether to join the fight for democracy.

After Pearl Harbor, Americans finally got the message about the mortal threat to their country. The United States went to war against the Axis and emerged victorious four years later.

By 1945, America seemed to have avenged Pearl Harbor, once and for all—at great human cost. And Americans everywhere agreed that the United States would never again suffer a deadly surprise attack.

———■◇■———

As it turned out, however, there would be more Pearl Harbors.

On September 11, 2001, many years after I

took—and promptly failed—my fifth-grade math quiz, another brazen attack came out of the blue and stole the lives of thousands of Americans. This time, it was close to home. I watched from a pier on the west side of Manhattan as the Twin Towers collapsed, killing nearly three thousand people. The acrid smell from the wreckage filled my nose for weeks afterward.

The newspaper headlines the next morning made no mistake of it, calling the terrorist attacks of September 11 a "second Pearl Harbor."

Almost twenty years after that, when I first decided to write this book, the United States had come under assault from a different kind of foe, an invisible and lethal virus that seemed to strike without warning. During that terrible spring of 2020, the surgeon general of the United States announced, "This is going to be our Pearl Harbor moment."

All of these Pearl Harbors had something in common. Despite what seemed (in retrospect) like obvious warning signs, America found itself unprepared, and there was finger-pointing at those people inside the country who, it was believed, allowed this to occur. And in each case, racism—toward the Japanese after Pearl Harbor, toward Muslims after 9/11, or toward China and Asian Americans when the COVID-19 pandemic struck—infected how some Americans decided to assign blame for what had happened.

Why, I asked myself, had the story of Pearl Harbor so powerfully shaped how we understand our present? Why is this history so *unsettled*?

Winston Churchill, the British politician who guided Great Britain through the worst days of World War II as prime minister, remarked that "Those that fail to learn from history are doomed to repeat it."

How should we react when our world changes suddenly? Do we give up or do we dig in and fight back? Do we look for scapegoats, someone to blame, or do we try to help one another?

The real story of Pearl Harbor, it turns out, is more complicated—and much more interesting, tragic, and heroic—than the simplified version handed down to us by our parents and grandparents.

I wrote *Attacked!* to try to get past the headlines, the official memories, and the REMEMBER PEARL HARBOR posters, to tell a story from the words, memories, and experiences of a diverse cast of characters, ordinary people who could never have prepared for a morning when history came crashing out of a blue sky.

CHAPTER 1

Only a few weeks into the most important mission of his life, Takeo Yoshikawa—code name: "Morimura"—had run out of ideas. It was the fall of 1941, and the twenty-eight-year-old Japanese spy was supposed to be gathering as much information as possible about the sprawling American naval base at Pearl Harbor, an enormous, closely guarded military installation on the Hawaiian island of Oahu.

Posing as a Japanese diplomat, Yoshikawa expected to move freely through the city of Honolulu and its surrounding towns. But all of Oahu felt like an armed camp, with military police manning every street corner. As he jostled against strangers on crowded sidewalks, he felt watched. Unfamiliar sounds and voices trailed out of streetcars, bars, pool halls, and shops of every type, and hundreds of American sailors in crisp white uniforms spilled onto the streets at all hours. Yoshikawa scurried past them, avoiding eye contact.

Every night, in the secret code room of the Japanese consulate where Yoshikawa worked undercover, the telegraph machine spewed questions and demands for information.

"How many naval vessels are docked?"

"Where are the battleships and aircraft carriers anchored?"

"How many aircraft are stationed at Ford Island?"

If he didn't deliver answers, it would mean shame for Yoshikawa and for his proud parents.

Yoshikawa had grown up in a family that prized military training. In high school, he was a champion swordsman of kendo, the stick-fighting sport that had helped train samurai warriors for centuries. He followed the tenets of Zen Buddhism and believed that its teachings of self-discipline prepared him well for the fight against Japan's enemies.

He had entered the Imperial Japanese Naval Academy just two years before Japan's fateful decision to become a true empire.

Imperial Japan—*Dai Nippon Teikoku*. The island nation of 100 million people had changed faster than any other country in history. Once the territory of medieval samurai lords known as shogun, Japan had morphed into an industrial powerhouse in mere decades.

At a time when European and American empires had carved up Africa and much of Asia, Japan was determined to compete with the great world powers.

In 1931, the Japanese army crossed the Sea of Japan and invaded resource-rich Manchuria, renaming it Manchukuo. Six years later, in 1937, Japan staged an all-out, brutal invasion of China. Blessed by the emperor himself, the war in China became known as "the sacred war," or *seisen*. Many Japanese citizens believed firmly that their country's military conquests were a righteous quest for glory.

On December 13, 1937, Japanese troops captured the Chinese city of Nanjing and slaughtered as many as 300,000 soldiers and civilians. Western news reports of the atrocities shocked many Americans, turning public opinion in the United States sharply against Japan's new push into Asia.

Japan pressed on with its war aims. Under the rallying cry of "Asia for Asians," Japan announced what it called the Greater East Asia Co-Prosperity Sphere (under Japanese leadership). Japanese propaganda criticized Western powers for their own imperialism in Asia—and the United States for its racist treatment of its citizens of color, particularly those of Asian descent. But in reality, these messages covered up Japan's ruthless treatment of the Asian peoples newly under its control.

Japan soon joined with Nazi Germany and Fascist Italy, forming a military pact in September 1940. Each country in the Axis pledged to go to war to protect the others.

As Japan's military chiefs dreamed of an empire spanning the Pacific, they saw only one real obstacle: a single US naval base in a shallow harbor, bristling with battleships, aircraft carriers, and thousands of American sailors. No other military force in the Pacific had the strength—or was close enough—to block Japan's ambitions.

Japan's military leaders decided they needed to know more about what its main enemy across the Pacific was up to. They sent an unassuming, slightly nervous young spy to find out.

The spy Takeo Yoshikawa in an undated photo.

On Yoshikawa's first attempt to get a closer look at the big naval base at Pearl Harbor, his taxi driver sped up as they passed the wrought-iron perimeter fence. He explained to Yoshikawa that the Navy was on the lookout for spies, and that police officers lurked in the bushes to arrest anyone—even an innocent cabdriver—trying to peer inside.

The Navy wasn't taking chances: on nearby Hickam Field air base, where hundreds of America's best fighter aircraft were parked close together out in the open, armed guards stood by to protect them from potential sneak attacks by Japanese secret agents. The Navy's commanders reasoned that they would be safest this way.

If the Americans found out who Yoshikawa really was, it would be life in prison—or death by firing squad.

———◆———

After a particularly stressful day, Yoshikawa made his way up to the Shunchoro Teahouse in Alewa Heights in Honolulu, to relax over whiskies and soda.

It was a beautiful evening, and the Shunchoro's main room had a large picture window looking out toward the ocean. Laid out before Yoshikawa was an unobstructed view of the US Navy base at Pearl Harbor. "Lights were flickering all over," he later remarked, "making it look like an enormous starfish."

That very evening, a new plan took shape in Yoshikawa's mind.

Although Hawaii was an American territory, much of it was culturally Japanese. While tourist brochures touted Hawaii as a vacation paradise for white visitors, two-thirds of the island's 260,000 full-time residents were descended from Japanese parents or grandparents—men and women who had immigrated to pick pineapples or cut sugarcane on large plantations where thousands of poorly paid workers toiled in the hot sun.

With the right disguise, Yoshikawa realized, he could blend in.

Donning a Hawaiian shirt and cap, the spy began to make daily forays onto the streets of Honolulu, listening for bits and pieces of information about the US fleet.

He went swimming, making note of coral reefs that might prevent a boat from reaching the shore safely.

He read the local papers, carefully clipping information about admirals, captains... and their ships.

Abandoning his diplomatic cover, he sometimes worked as a dishwasher at the Pearl Harbor officers' club, pricking up his ears for gossip.

He played the tourist, taking glass-bottom boat tours, going on hikes, and even purchasing tickets for charter flights that offered a view of all of Oahu from several thousand feet up.

He took measurements of the harbor depth, breathing through a reed to stay underwater for long periods of time without attracting attention.

And he returned again and again to the Shunchoro Teahouse. He even took to renting a room with a clear view of the harbor, which he would scan carefully through a set of binoculars. Under the spy's watchful gaze, planes took off and landed, and ships of all sizes came and went.

All of this information he committed to memory, never carrying a camera, pen, or notepad. At night, in the cramped telegraph room in the consulate, he would carefully encode his daily catch of information and wire it to Tokyo.

Over weeks and months, Yoshikawa assembled a detailed picture of every military installation on Oahu—including all the ships stationed in Pearl Harbor. He could even predict their movements with accuracy.

But he could not answer one simple question: Why did his bosses in Tokyo need all this information?

ABOUT THE AUTHOR

Marc Favreau is the acclaimed author of *Crash: The Great Depression and the Fall and Rise of America*, *Spies: The Secret Showdown Between America and Russia*, *Attacked! Pearl Harbor and the Day War Came to America*, and (with Michael Eric Dyson) *Unequal: A Story of America*. Favreau is also the director of editorial projects at the New Press. He lives with his family in Martha's Vineyard, Massachusetts.

HISTORY AS YOU'VE NEVER READ IT BEFORE

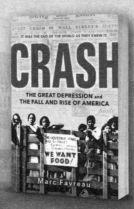

FROM ACCLAIMED AUTHOR
MARC FAVREAU